TEACHING
IN THE
SLUM SCHOOL

MERRILL'S
INTERNATIONAL EDUCATION SERIES

Under the Editorship of

KIMBALL WILES

Dean of the College of Education

University of Florida

TEACHING
IN THE
SLUM SCHOOL

ROBERT D. STROM

The Ohio State University   87021

CHARLES E. MERRILL BOOKS, INC.

Columbus, Ohio

Library of Congress Catalog Card Number: 65–21162

First printing ....*June, 1965*
Second printing ....*March, 1966*

PRINTED IN THE UNITED STATES OF AMERICA

To

Shirley

and

Steven

Preface

As the focus of current national attention, urban slums represent an issue of great importance, a complex of problems, a context for commitment. Never before have the economic, educational and social dimensions of lower-class neighborhoods been so visible to the general public as they are today. In part this is because American society can ill afford to remain myopic about a growing culture of poverty in its midst. However, our primary motivation for assisting the poor is not merely to avoid widespread dependency nor diminish the number of human obstacles to social progress. Rather, it is widely believed that we now have within our power the ability to translate long-standing ideals into practice. We are now able to ensure the promise of equal opportunity as engendered in our political creeds, to make real the prospect of dignity for every citizen, and to render success more likely in the quest of each man for security.

Certainly education has a major role in effecting the change from what life is to what it can be for millions of inner-city youngsters. Therefore, beginning teachers in slum schools are the principal audience for whom this writing is intended. My attempt has been to present an overview of important concerns which can influence failure or progress in the classroom. Evidence seems to indicate that success in working with children of the poor requires understanding of low-income life, knowledge regarding the school role in serving an unstructured community, cognizance about functions and strengths of supportive staff members, and familiarity with learning types, styles and pace. These respective issues form a major portion of the content.

Another expected audience of readers are those whose work indirectly affects pupil growth. This group includes professional staff of teacher training institutions, special services faculty, members of communal, fraternal or educational organizations. There is much that we who are outside of classrooms can do to provide instructors with the kinds of support needed to render pupil prospect more hopeful, instructional effectiveness more likely, teacher role more realistic and satisfying. Thus, a portion of this book contains recommendations for the consideration of those individuals and agencies desiring to improve their measure and method of fostering education in urban slums.

Admittedly, the mood of this text is optimistic. My experience in working with teachers of the slum would render any other emphasis untenable. There is much our profession can be proud of in some classrooms of low-income districts; there is also much which remains to be done. Our time has been chosen for the task.

Robert D. Strom

Columbus, Ohio

Table of Contents

TEACHING
IN THE
SLUM SCHOOL

> *If a free society cannot help the many
> who are poor, it cannot save the few who
> are rich.*
>
> —*John F. Kennedy*

The Slumdwellers

1

Within the central complex of many major cities reside the slum-dwellers. At least two-thirds of them are Negro, Puerto Rican, Mexican American, or members of some other minority group. Many are newcomers, domestic immigrants from rural defeat who have fled to the city in search of its elusive advantages. They say they will return to the farm tomorrow; history says they are here to stay. A large segment of the adult population have experienced family disruption and the marital crises of separation or divorce. Some are attempting to build their second or third set of hopes; to others, time has taught the futility of dreams, aspiration, and initiative.

More by circumstance than choice, the slum family is usually managed by a woman. Uneducated and unskilled, seldom able to qualify for a job, and frustrated in attempts to resolve financial difficulties, the father is apt to turn to liquor, gambling, or other pursuits that ensure his habitual absence from the home. These misdeeds by the male parent are compounded by their added strain upon the family's already precarious balance between income and expense. His infrequent homecomings are seldom cause for celebration; instead, he is likely to be greeted with maternal reports of child misconduct and the expectation by all that due physical punishment will prevail.

For the young, their "old man" tends to become a desultory police official whom they may fear but find difficult to love. Lacking daily contact with the home, fathers may not understand youngsters and often are unable to influence them wisely. The usual result is a transfer of actual if not titular headship to the mother.

While maternal influence is dominant in the majority of slum homes, it is the only influence in many others. Though the 2.3 million families composed solely of a mother and her children represent only one twelfth of all families with youngsters, they make up more than a fourth of all families classified as poor. Together with mothers who live with their children as a subfamily in the home of a relative, these women are raising nearly six million children (1). The dilemma is aggravated by the fact that legal marriage is not as likely to occur in slums as elsewhere, so that separation of parents less often results in a mother being left with the benefit of formal financial support.

The most universal problem shared by those who assume responsibility for individual slum families is an inadequate wage. Often subsisting on annual incomes of less than $3,000, these households are unable to meet their own needs and become known as chronically dependent. One study, for example, shows that 6 percent of the families in St. Paul, Minnesota, suffered from such a compounding of problems that they absorbed over half the community's services (2). For an adult, one of the psychological consequences of such problems can be to produce feelings of futility and bitterness which in themselves interfere with self-advancement.

More important, however, is the effect on children. Family poverty means that for one-fourth of all school-aged children in this country, the gates of opportunity will be closed; their future promises to be no better than and probably worse than their past; they are victims of an environmental trap that threatens to impose upon them a lifetime devoid of dignity. For slum children, poverty in adulthood appears an almost certain legacy. This situation did not exist in the past. At one time the poor were not only those able to earn little or nothing: a fair number would eventually improve their lot. But as demands for higher education and more technical skills increasingly upgrade our labor force, the ranks of the poor will be reserved for those families with heads unable or not permitted to qualify for better paying jobs—the nonwhite, the rural immigrant, the unskilled woman; in short, the slumdweller.

HIGH COST OF BAD HOUSING

Winston Churchill once said: "We shape our buildings and afterwards our buildings shape us." Without doubt, the housing one occupies can influence health, attitude, and behavior, especially if the residence is inadequate. This is not to imply that good quarters will create a satisfying home but that bad housing makes it easy for the home to fail and difficult to succeed. The poor family that is forced to inhabit a place lacking in space or facility is undermined in every aspect of life. Proper privacy is denied, family clashes are fostered, normal parent-child relationship becomes more difficult, slovenly habits are stimulated, and a sense of shame smothers family loyalty. It is not surprising that the slum family is in quest of a suitable dwelling place.

Though more often affected by ill-housing than others, low-income families are least in a position to effect change in their type of residence. Paradoxically, the incentive for slum landlords, because of property taxes, is to refrain from improving the living conditions of their tenants. Tax laws and condemnation procedures combine with the peculiarly vulnerable situation of those who are poor to pay the most for the worst housing. Among the factors which operate in this fashion are the municipal property tax, capital gains tax, the basis for appraising value in condemnation, and the depreciation allowance.

The property tax, based as it is upon valuation, increases as property is improved. Numerous studies conclude that such a basis for this tax leads to property neglect in slum districts (3). The same owner response is produced by a capital gains tax. While resale in neighborhoods of middle income may depend on maintenance, in the slum it is more likely to depend on land value and net income. Therefore, ultimate profit lies in simply retaining land until it becomes valuable in current standards. Condemnation procedures provide one of the reasons that income production determines resale value. Even though income is not a consideration in setting the property tax, it is recognized as a factor in negotiating payment upon condemnation. For this reason too, money spent on maintenance produces little cash benefit for the landlord.

Maintenance is also affected by the depreciation allowance, whereby real estate is treated much like machinery. That is to say, a high percentage of depreciation may be written off during the early years, gradually decreasing as time passes. Though a single owner may not receive credit for more than his own cost, upon resale the property may be depreciated all over again. Hence, the depreciation allowance encourages quick sales and large profits in early years, unlike the capital gains tax, which leads to holding on for an increase in property value. Both provisions have in common, however, that they return no profit for the cost of maintaining or improving slum property. Maximum profit lies in manipulating tax and financial matters quite unrelated to building maintenance; it also lies in securing high *short-term profit,* which translates into placing the most tenants feasible in the space available with lowest possible expenditure (4).

In sum, one of the great problems of the slumdweller is that he must contribute to the profit of new owners each time a tenement changes hands. As a building gets older, each new price paid for it represents more profit taking in the preceding sale; in turn, the dying building has more and more tenants crowded into it to meet costs, thus hastening its dilapidation.

Given this circumstance, what happens to slumdwellers should be obvious—they overpay. Many slum families spend more than 30 percent of their income on rent to secure a sufficiently large, though perhaps inadequate tenement. (Inadequate housing in this sense refers to an absence of one of the three plumbing facilities—running water, bath, and exclusive use of toilet.) Where money to obtain space is unavailable, some families reluctantly break up. Of 11,500 children who were in New York City foster care homes during 1960, at one point 750 could have gone home immediately had adequate low-cost housing been available to their parents (5).

A sizable number of families, more in hope than confidence, await admission to the healthful apartments of public housing. Unfortunately, fewer than a million of these units exist, accommodating less than 3 million of the 35 million who are poor. In Washington, D.C., the number of families waiting to be admitted has at times exceeded the total number of units. That such quarters are badly needed can be shown by many statistics, one of which disclosed that of more than 3,000 illegitimate offspring whose parents received Aid for Dependent Children in Cleveland, Ohio, only 10 percent lived in public housing while 90 percent occupied overcrowded tenement flats (6).

Sooner or later, numerous families realize they can no longer pay rent and meet other living costs; consequently, they turn to the most efficient way of meeting expenses, that of sharing quarters with others. Only by doubling up with kinsmen or neighbors can bills be paid and competition for space remain possible. This procedure is the norm among Negro families, who, as shown by studies in Baltimore (7), Newark (8), and Chicago (9), must pay significantly more than whites for equivalent housing. It is easy to see why low income Negro families are listed as being substantially larger than their white counterparts. Indeed, in some cities the percentage of families that are crowded (more than one person per room) may be two to four times as high for Negroes than for whites. For all slumdwellers, but particularly for the Negro, it is costly to be poor.

THE EXTENDED FAMILY

The economic necessity of occupying crowded quarters results in what might be called an *extended family,* a common social unit within slum neighborhoods. Dissimilar in size and structure from the usual American household, the extended family tends to have a unique effect upon the personal development of its members. Among the psychological consequences likely to occur in crowded living conditions are the following: lack of self-sufficiency, destruction of illusions, mental strain, and the inability to make decisions.

Persistent crowding from early life seems to affect adversely the self-sufficiency of slum children, their ability to be alone, and their sense of individuality. To foster such attributes young people need periods of time by themselves, chances to play alone, occasions of seclusion in a place of their choosing. However, with few if any opportunities for privacy, young slumdwellers come to feel incomplete and uneasy when not in the presence of others. Thus, in all of their activities, they seek situations in which other people are present, whether it be in the hallway, the street, or the movies. Constantly looking outside oneself for stimulation tends to diminish any prospect of introspection or looking within for the satisfactions of life. Having been denied privacy and the development of an interest in solitary pursuits, these children cannot be expected to engage easily in the kind of study habits required for success in school.

Crowding also serves to destroy illusions which children build about other people. There is a point of contact beyond which illusion stands the hazard of complete destruction. In the mechanism of illusion one projects into an individual qualities that the viewer would like to find there instead of accepting what is actual. Ordinarily the process of disillusion must come with better acquaintance and frequent contact. Only in this way can people be seen as they are rather than on dress parade or as the viewer would have them. As slum children are brought into unavoidable contact with adult weakness and greed, they tend to find it difficult to build identification with their parents or other adult models in the community. Personal experience is likely to make them cynical about people, organization and government. Each of us idealizes out of dream material, but the clatter and push of crowded slum living appears to easily awaken its membership.

If slumdwellers lack the benefit of some illusions, their circumstances provide for others. Image goals and hero worship are common but in a depersonalized form so that the name of an eminent individual stands not for personal attributes of character or personality except for abstractions such as power, high averages or victory in sports. In other words, from his intimate experience with personal deception, the slum child has learned that he cannot afford to worship a person as such. Those whom he most admires, of course, are people who because of their physical prowess have overcome the circumstance of adversity (10).

Absence of illusion also results in what some might call realism, a clearness of vision or perception regarding the motives of others. This enables slum children to see both what is good and bad in people; how else can we understand the ability of these youngsters to perceive love that lies behind harsh hands or voice? This sensitivity to the motives of others has implications for classroom rapport and discipline; it often enables him to perceive the true motives of his teachers. The slum child's ability to discern the motivation of adult behavior may, to be sure, break brittle idols, but it often gives him strength and a sense of belongingness in the face of what might seem to an objective outsider to be unreasonable and cruel treatment.

A third effect of crowding is mental strain, commonly shown in irritability and negativism. City dwellers at any income level are uncomfortably aware of crowding—on the bus and subway, on the highway, at lunch hour in the cafeteria, or on hot days in the park. In these situations everyone feels the strain of having to adjust to others for a period of time. In the slum, however, we see children who have never known any other mode of existence.

Mental strain arises from always having to "hold onto oneself." Each of us builds walls about the ego to preserve its sanctity from prying eyes. That these are walls of fear seems certain, and watchful guardianship over them cannot be relaxed so long as others are about. So in the slum one meets large numbers of adults and some children who want to get away from everyone they know in order to find a surcease from this eternal vigilance. The results, when periods of freedom are lacking, are either a forbidding negativism or irritable temper outbursts which belong to the phenomenon of fatigue. The fatigue phenomenon seems to derive from constant failure to be free of the task of guarding one's status-preserving walls. As the suburban solution of summer retreat or travel are beyond the means of slumdwellers, the usual procedure is to stay away from home as much as possible or to keep late hours. Little wonder some children are tired in school or preoccupied by autistic thinking, daydreaming in an attempt to shut out the crowded external world.

In some of these children one can observe a constantly recurring picture of touchy reactions and irritability as the personality is pressed. It is as though nerves have been frayed by the constant effort of adjusting to others, the continuous challenge to the integrity of one's defenses. A lumberman jumping from log to log unable to take a moment for rest would present the same picture if he were never allowed to relax—and these children are never allowed to relax. Even the nights conspire to this end as others crowd close—sleeping three to five in a bed—so that even during periods of slumber there must be an awareness of the imminence of others and the compromise and surrender this entails.

Another outcome of crowding is that it tends to thwart the development of deliberative or decision-making abilities. Seldom is choice a major factor in slum living. Even personal preference for interaction is affected by crowding because contact is predetermined by space. For some, there is no possibility of governing either in kind or in amount their involvement with neighbors or other members of the extended family. Even in personal relations, circumstance is often the deciding factor and leads many slumdwellers to a position of resignation, apathy or fatalism insofar as control over the direction of events is concerned. For young girls the high degree of sexual stimulation produced by crowding may lead, in certain cases, to expression after a torturous course through repression, boredom and discontent. Those who do not react this way may reject sexuality categorically, defending themselves with one problem or another.

It is natural for the crowded poor to feel driven by fate as they lack money, contacts, attitudes—all those requisites necessary to register change. With few alternatives for action at home, children from this environment find it difficult to undertake any deliberative or decision-making tasks assigned in the classroom. Their inability to generalize, combined with their propensity to languor in deliberation and to delay in declaring preferences, puts them at a disadvantage, especially on speed-oriented tests. Option is foreign to them and becomes particularly difficult when they are confronted with more than two alternatives, as in the case of multiple-choice examinations. Often the motivation to inquire, to demonstrate curiosity, has been retarded by experience at home where the stock reply to all questions of cause has been, "Because I said so. . . . That's the way it is."

LIFE IN THE STREET

Where great inadequacy of space exists, family members frequently spend a large amount of time out of doors. This has serious implications as far as children are concerned, for what they see on the streets will affect their values, negate or reinforce parental example. On sidewalks, midst tumbledown porches, or in garbage-filled alleys, youngsters will undoubtedly observe the language and action accompanying gambling, narcotics, drinking and prostitution. In the street, children may have for their emulation those from whom all hope and dignity have fled, in whom the human spirit has withered away. How influential such examples will be in individual cases depends on circumstance and therefore is unpredictable; we can predict, however, that in many cases the lessons of the street will be a child's most effective, if not positive, mentor.

Street life affects child life in other ways. Not within parental reach or control, peer groups are likely to be formed at an earlier age among children in slums than in suburbs and will tend to assume greater control of individual behavior. As one mother put it, "It's hard to supervise a kid's play from the fifth floor." Studies of low-income families in Washington, D.C., suggest strikingly early cutoff points in parental control of progeny. As early as age six, children in some homes seem to seize control (11). One can hardly overlook the relevance of such a pattern to the fact that they cannot reasonably be kept in the house.

CHILD REARING

Though life in the streets is largely subject to the control of peer groups, responsibility for child rearing is ostensibly assumed by one of several generation groups within the extended family—the *elderly* (grandparents, aunts, uncles, over-age parents); the *middle-aged* and *younger adult* (parents); and finally, children may be reared wholly or in part by *other children,* usually older sisters and brothers. Both the type and effect of encouragement, counsel, punishment, example, and affection given the young will vary, depending much on which of these age groups occupies the dominant role in child rearing.

In nations other than our own, more cultural uniformity and a slower rate of progress have allowed maintenance of close adult-adolescent relationships. In contrast, the rapidity of change in America, in rendering child life today so much different than a few years ago, tends to lessen the experiences young and old have had in common. This separates persons of different generations and makes the task of grandparents who are charged with bringing up the young more difficult. Yet even in the slum, where elders are more likely to assume child rearing tasks than in other segments of society, they can, if patient and tactful, bring the best of the past into close rapport with the eagerness of youth. The cherished values and mores of "the good old days" appear more worthy of consideration to children when the life of its advocates is pleasant and unimposing. On the other hand, when elders have a past of frustrated hopes and bitter experience, undesirable values may be transmitted to children. A pathological distrust of people usually results in an attempt to force the same attitude on children as a guide for social relations. Usually this creates rebellion by one's charges and a rejection of authority.

When raising their own children, slum parents differ slightly from grandparents in their point of vantage. Standing in a different place in the life cycle, their view is less one of retrospect and rather emphasizes futurity. To young mothers and fathers, the past is incidental, life is an open book, and the next chapter may be better. Usually the younger the parent, the more they are striving (still hoping to get out of the slum), if not for themselves, for their children. Both grandparents and parents are alike, however, in their authoritative approach, for age supposedly has learned and is positive about many things which make for impatience with children, their young eagerness to experiment and test limits and their sacrilege of the quiet life.

Misbehavior is usually not followed by a withholding of privileges, for few exist; nor is more supervision applied, for this is often impossible; lectures of reason are not administered. Fear of physical punishment—wherein mother acts as informant and judge, father as executioner for chastisement—is the prevailing motivation to evoke appropriate behavior. As family size increases, there is a greater tendency to manage by rule than by decision in an individual case. Whereas in a family of few children, problems can be dealt with on individual merit as they arise, in a large family there is a greater necessity to make rules from which deviation is not tolerated.

The third type of child rearing, whereby older brothers and sisters serve as parent substitutes for the younger, obtains in many slum families and in societies where life is simple. Sometimes siblings carry adult authority; in other instances, only responsibility. In either case, sibling child care in many low-income households is the most realistic in essence because the young understand the young, see their problems through youthful eyes, measure difficulties by the criteria of their own needs. They know too which measures are effective and which must be avoided. Because the charges have confidence in their kinsmen, they are responsive to the chosen discipline, especially since it is usually in line with peer standards. In one study, 90 percent of the children show a higher degree of acceptance for the discipline advanced by older brothers and sisters than by parents (12).

Many children of poverty report their elder peers to be better teachers than their parents, more able to understand how hard it is to learn something new. The older children, who have recently been through a given learning process themselves, are more patient, more ready and able to speak on the student's level. They do not push, frighten and frustrate as adults frequently do. Also, siblings have no vested interest that would result in unrealistic expectation.

Unfortunately, the role of older children in a slum home has negative consequences as well. To be sure, one could argue that the experience of rearing younger children develops habits of responsibility and service to others, and hastens maturity and adult behavior. But where children are many and their births extended over a period of time, the eldest are exploited in a surrogate function and thus are forced to grow up before their time, to accelerate their biology, to forego their own child life and adolescence, to simulate adulthood. Moreover, when crises befall the family, older children are sacrificed to the common need. The device most often used to improve family income is to send an additional member to work—this is the eldest slum child, still a child but older than his siblings, expected to be a man before he has been a boy (13).

From whatever vantage slums are seen, the picture is depressing (14). Obviously the image presented here is *modal* and therefore cannot be expected to reflect the lives of *all* slumdwellers even though in the main it would apply. Until recently, societal response to the conditions under which these people live was one of either anger or pity, assuming that slums were incurable, even unavoidable. Today, however, a new national view has emerged, a new attitude prevails, as exemplified in President Johnson's declaration of war on poverty: "Our national goal is to provide every citizen with the opportunity to advance his welfare to the limits of his capacities." In effect, this means the poor cannot be abandoned to their problems; disadvantaged children must not become disabled adults; slumdwellers must be restored to useful city life.

RESOURCES

(1)   Orshansky, Mollie, "Children of the Poor," *Social Security Bulletin,* U.S. Department of Health, Education and Welfare (Washington, D.C.: Government Printing Office, July 1963), p. 9.

(2)   Shorr, Alvin L., *Slums and Social Insecurity* (Washington, D.C.: Government Printing Office, 1963), p. 75.

(3)   Walker, Mable, "Tax Responsibility for the Slum," *Tax Policy,* Vol. XXVI, No. 10 (October 1959).

(4)   Hearings before the Committee on Ways and Means, House of
      Representatives, 87th Cong., 1st sess., on the tax recommendations
      of the President contained in his message transmitted to the Con-
      gress, Apr. 20, 1961, May 12, 15, 16, 17, 18 and 19, 1961. U.S.
      Government Printing Office, Washington, D.C., Vol. 2, p. 955.

(5)   Dumpson, James R., "The Economy of Adequate Service," *Child
      Welfare,* Vol. 39, No. 10 (December 1960), p. 5.

(6)   Cuyahoga County Welfare Department, "Ill-Starred Children,"
      Annual Report, 1959, Ohio.

(7)   Millspaugh, Martin, and Gurney Breckenfeld, *The Human Side
      of Urban Renewal,* ed. by Miles Colean (Baltimore, Md.: Fight-
      Blight Inc., 1958), 233 pp.

(8)   Gottmann, Jean, *Megalopolis* (New York: The Twentieth Century
      Fund, 1961), p. 709.

(9)   Duncan, Beverly, and Philip M. Hauser, *Housing a Metropolis—
      Chicago* (Glencoe, Ill.: The Free Press, 1960), p. 15.

(10) Plant, James S., "Family Living Space and Personality Develop-
      ment," in *A Modern Introduction to the Family,* eds. Norman W.
      Bell and Ezra F. Vogel (Glencoe, Ill.: The Free Press, 1960),
      pp. 510–20.

(11) Lewis, Hylan, "Child Rearing Among Low Income Families in the
      District of Columbia." Presented at the National Conference on
      Social Welfare, Minneapolis, Minnesota, May 16, 1961, mimeo-
      graphed.

(12) Bossard, James H. S., *Parent and Child: Studies in Family Behavior*
      (Philadelphia: University of Pennsylvania Press, 1953), Chap. V.

(13) Strom, Robert D., "What Is the School Speed-up Doing to Chil-
      dren?" *The Elementary School Journal,* Vol. 65, No. 4 (January
      1965), pp. 206–7.

(14) Strom, Robert D., "Are These Our Ugly Americans?" *Kentucky
      School Journal,* Vol. 43, No. 2 (October 1964), pp. 20–22, 46.

Expanding Role of Inner-City Schools

2

The school has changed perhaps more than any other institution in our time. In response to the knowledge explosion, there have been innovations in curriculum, methodology, materials, organization and teacher preparation. Currently serving students from the nursery through old age, some schools function day and evening during the entire year. In slum and suburb alike, education is now expected to solve the dilemma of unemployment and welfare, to ensure economic efficiency for its patrons, and to provide mental health for all.

At the same time, needs indigenous to local neighborhoods must be served. In this context, the role of slum schools has expanded to include surrogate responsibility for the very young, adjustment of the newcomer, conjunctive educational efforts with the home, and an interpretation of societal expectations and prospects for individual citizens. In turn, these represent new commitments to the child, his home, community and nation.

THE SURROGATE FUNCTION

Each year a large number of low-income children enter first grade with a complex of attitudes toward education that precludes learning;

13

a perception of the school that prohibits its purpose; and a view of society at large that threatens personal advance. Usually the result is early retardation, frustration, and failure. The ways in which these unprofitable attitudes are developed in the home have recently become the subject of considerable discussion and research.

At the University of Chicago, Robert Hess and others have considered the problem of maternal competence in preparing children for school (1). Since middle-class children for the most part come to school adequately prepared whereas their counterparts from poor families are ill-prepared, the problem was to determine what facilitating experiences are present in middle-class families that typically do not occur in lower socioeconomic homes. Through a series of questions and tasks directed to approximately 160 mothers and their four-year-old children representing the several income levels, investigators were able to glean some rather interesting data with regard to differences in maternal attitudes toward school, perception of educational purpose, and role in preparing children for learning.

One technique used by Hess to determine perception of school purpose was to ask each mother what she would say to her child on his first day of school. Although there were differences of response within class groups, a typical mother from the lower-income home said, "I tell him to do what the teacher says, not get into trouble, not to fight, to come home right after school, and not to get lost." This view of school raises issues of dealing with authority and peers rather than presenting educational content. If learning is mentioned, it is incidental or secondary. Such a response is in contrast to the middle-class parent who was likely to say, "The teacher is like Mommy, you learn from her; if you have trouble, go to her; you are going to learn to read and write." This approach views school activity in terms of the child's learning experiences.

The mothers were also asked to explain a picture of a teacher and mother in conference. Subjects from the low-income group most often said that the mother had been called in by the school regarding some disciplinary problem. Middle-class mothers more frequently saw the conference as one in which a parent was coming to consult with her child's teacher about a learning problem. The major difference between these two types of response is in the view of the school as an institution with which the child must cope, as contrasted with a view of the school as a place of learning. The lower-class child approaches school unoriented toward learning but attuned to a need of getting along with the institution. School experience is defined to him as a problem of adapting to the teacher and to the peer situation. This presents a misconception of school purpose, with a heavy emphasis upon conformity and physical behavior rather than mental activity.

To ascertain variations in styles of maternal instruction, each parent was asked to teach her child how to assemble a jigsaw puzzle. More often than not, the middle-class mother would indicate, "This is a jigsaw puzzle which makes a picture. We remove the pieces and then put them back together so that the picture is complete again. See where all the pieces are and look at the colors so you will know where they go." Thus, the task was defined; the child had been told how to proceed. Then, spilling out the pieces, the mother gave verbal directions and encouragement as her youngster worked on his task. Mothers of the low-income group, equally supportive of their children, often dumped the puzzle without verbal directions and said, "You do it." The only guidance offered was in the frequent phrase, "Turn it around, turn it around. . . ." Thirty-five times one mother said this, until finally, in defeat and frustration, her child replied, "You do it."

Although the mother of the frustrated child was trying to help her boy, she did not know how to teach and was unable to convey the concepts needed to solve his problem. The ability to communicate concepts, to share information, and to program a simple task is seldom present in the low-income family. However, this is not the only important outcome. Imagine the child in repeated interaction with his mother coming upon problems which he tries to solve but, through lack of maternal assistance, finds impossible. The reaction of defeat, "You do it," is likely to recur and be magnified many times, resulting in feelings of apathy and despair that some problems cannot be solved. Compare his response with that of the more favored middle-class child who did not know more than he about the puzzle to begin with but who through experience realized that with some guidance there was a way to reach a solution. Upon this kind of motivational base, positive attitudes toward new learning can emerge.

In the absence of positive paternal guidance for these children, one might hope the female parent could provide compensatory influence. Unfortunately, the facts are otherwise. Indeed, evidence most often points to an inadequacy in the cognitive features of early mother-child exchange that tends to foster later alienation from the educative processes and other basic institutions of society. The patterns of communication that develop between mother and child have a lasting effect upon the youngster's cognitive equipment, influencing what he attends to, how he interprets messages, and how he responds. These patterns are not always adaptive or functional for learning situations and may prevent a student from taking advantage of available classroom experiences.

The problem of inadequate patterns of communication between mother and child is exacerbated by adult unawareness of the need for children to have certain experiences in preparation for formal education. Many slum children have never been outside their neighborhood or city, to a zoo or park, in the woods, or on a lake. Research indicates that except for the genetic patterning of physical growth, a human self does not develop through the process of unfolding as some child development books dealing with levels and phases would suggest. Rather, a human self results from the processes of interacting and interrelating. It follows that the quality of self produced depends in large measure on the quality of interactions and relationships made available to the individual.

According to Benjamin Bloom, professor at the University of Chicago, the difference between a very favorable environment and an underprivileged environment may affect intellectual development each year in the first four of a child's life by about 2.5 I.Q. points per year or 10 I.Q. points over the four-year period. Between ages 8 and 17, extreme environments may have an effect of only .4 points per year. Dr. Bloom contends that the cumulative effect of environmental influence during the first 17 years is about 20 I.Q. points when contrasting deprived and abundant backgrounds as they exist in America today. Dorothea McCarthy (2) is able to describe some 17 studies showing that environmentally deprived children tend to enter school at a considerable disadvantage when compared with their age-mates from middle and upper classes.

The assumptions that intelligence is fixed and that its development is predetermined by the genes is no longer tenable, writes J. Hunt at the University of Illinois. The fixed intelligence concept has resulted in educators overlooking the importance of experience at preschool level. Hunt cites research indicating that ability and readiness of parents to answer children's questions and to show affection-approval can make a difference in intelligence. He concludes that we must discover ways to govern the encounters children have with their environments, especially during the early years, in order that as adults they will have higher intellectual capacities than would otherwise be the case (3).*

In an attempt to compensate for the constricted life-space in which slum children must function, educators in Chicago, Baltimore, New York and other large cities have initiated programs of prekindergarten enrichment designed to include a dimension of experiences which are comparable to the background usually brought to school by students of middle class. Essentially these efforts resemble Maria Montessori's school for poor children, the Casa Dei Bambini, begun in Rome over half a century ago. Just as the purpose of Montessori's Roman venture was to make learning enjoyable in a prepared environment and to overcome home conditions that might foster alienation and failure in school, so too the focus of contemporary preschool experiments is on removing academic handicaps which might otherwise confront boys and girls upon entering the elementary grades. Youngsters of age three to four are for the first time being exposed to music, art and books; they are learning size, number and time concepts. They are being prepared for a more adequate chance to compete successfully later in formal academic situations.

Though the matter of kindergarten content remains a subject of dispute, this important element of education in the slum is also enjoying more acceptance than ever before. Currently endorsed by the National Education Association, the White House Conference on Education, and the Council of Chief State School Officers, public kindergartens presently enroll about 53 percent of the nation's five year olds. As important as this concept of preparing for grade school is to all, it has special significance in neighborhoods of low income where parents seldom plan or otherwise arrange events from which the young may profit. Because most inner-city teachers can attest to the increasing need for and effectiveness of early informal education, they strongly favor the surrogate role.

---

* From *The Tragic Migration* by Robert D. Strom, pp. 6–8, 13. Copyright 1964, National Education Association. Reprinted by permission.

ADJUSTMENT OF THE NEWCOMER

Each year 40 million Americans move. For some schools this means an increased number of pupils transferring into already over-crowded classrooms. Nevertheless, in most cases, records are quickly processed and education continues. This is not so in slum neighbor-hoods where the so-called newcomer seldom arrives with scholastic records or any background information. Coming primarily from rural and Southern regions, these recent immigrants to the big city present educators with some rather perplexing problems. In the ab-sence of biographical data, the decision regarding initial grade placement of the newcomer sometimes rests on extrinsic factors such as age or size. These indices do not take into account academic retardation and, therefore, can have the effect of inducing immediate frustration, humiliation, and alienation.

However, the problem is not confined to grade placement. It should be obvious that teaching cannot effectively proceed and appropriate learning processes will not occur in courses where an instructor is unfamiliar with the academic, emotional, familial, and social history of each class member. Experience in working with schools on the devel-opment and use of cumulative records suggests that the following scope of facts is needed to ensure optimum instruction: develop-mental history; medical, health and growth information; interpersonal relationships at home; cultural background and socioeconomic status; interaction with peers; test scores of aptitude and achievement; illustrative samples of school work; and observational information such as use of mental processes, attitudes, conduct, values, goals, talents, abilities, adjustment problems, and adjustive patterns. None of this information is ordinarily available about the slum newcomer.

For a time, development of a complex system of record exchange appeared to be the only alternative. A maze of administrative obstacles arose, however, to make this proposition untenable. Then, in 1962, in their booklet *Education and the Disadvantaged American,* the Educational Policies Commission of the National Education Associa-tion suggested the following possibility: "One way to deal with this problem is to enroll new pupils in an ungraded reception class pend-ing decision as to their proper place in school" (4). From this proposal have arisen several programs which merit commendation.

For example, in Los Angeles, where over 100,000 pupil transfers are recorded annually, a project known as the Reception Room has been established in two inner-city elementary schools. The two institutions were selected because they have the highest turnover in the city, with 20 to 25 children entering each week. Most of these children arrive with no school records or background data. In order to facilitate placement and orientation, a full-time teacher for remedial instruction, a full-time testing counselor, and a part-time child welfare and attendance worker for family case work and referral are available to each school. Close contact is maintained with health and welfare departments, church groups and charitable agencies so that, if home visits indicate a need, the immediate prospect of food, clothing, or medical service can be arranged.

Uprooted from familiar surroundings, newcomers naturally experience an acute sense of physical and social isolation, so that a seeming myriad of difficulties confront them in their attempt to adjust to the complexities of child rearing and homemaking in an urban environment. Consequently, the Milwaukee Public Schools operate an inmigrant program wherein youngsters and parents alike are carefully welcomed to the community and given any orientation or assistance possible. The practice of extending help and friendship when it is most needed has been proven a significant influence in bringing home and school closer together.

The importance of establishing harmony between the family and the school cannot be overemphasized, especially where the newcomer's former way of life substantially differed from city residence and its urban demands. The tug between the old and the new way of life is bound to show itself in the home. Usually the parents are reluctant to adjust, while the young are forced to acclimate themselves to new modes of behavior. This creation of a gulf between parent and child constitutes a grave social problem. Although the child can adjust by outward appearances, this is seldom done without expense to his social development because of antagonistic contact between the culture of the home and that of the school. At school the pupil is taught one thing, at home another, until the pupil finds it difficult to commit himself absolutely to either of his contending environments. Perhaps he changes his demeanor to that of the school and ridicules the mores, customs, and manners of his home. Then, in regret for hurting his parents, he may renounce the school. Inconsistency of conduct makes it impossible for him to hold steadfastly either to sympathies for school or affectionate regard for parents. Choices between home and school should not have to be made and need not be made when an effective program is operative to help inmigrants make their transition to useful city living.

CONJUNCTIVE HOME-SCHOOL EFFORTS

Important as they are, preschool and inmigrant programs cannot ensure pupil progress. Sometimes these efforts are neutralized in households where education lacks support and reinforcement. Indeed, there are instances in which familial influence tends to defeat the purpose of school. One of the more recent studies corroborating this misfortune comes from the special reading lab in San Francisco, where a feeling on the part of some pupils that learning to read well, or to read at all, is worthless, was traced to families where there is constant repetition of the theme that no matter how well a student does, he will never be allowed by society to practice his skills (5). That such an environment tends to diminish both aspiration and growth of its young is obvious. Consequently, the school goal of establishing conjunctive educational efforts with the home is receiving wide support and high priority for slum neighborhoods.

Unlike other holders of joint responsibility for human welfare, parent and teacher spend little time together in mapping strategies, sharing information and planning for a child's well-being, despite the fact that both have a genuine interest in the child, are committed to his development, and claim to seek the best help available where his welfare is concerned. Often the interchange of ideas between classroom and home is limited to several written or verbal communiqués per year. This problem is not unique to the slum but is more prevalent here. How two or three adults, parents and teacher, who share such a regard for and investment in the same child have so little to do with one another is difficult to accept if not to understand.

To be sure, low-income parents less often exhibit the exuberant cooperation with school personnel that one might expect to prevail in suburban communities. However, it is more important to understand why this is so than to use the fact as an indictment. Many slum

parents feel that the school is a closed system to which they are out-
siders; that to be a good parent, one is expected to remain at home
and not bother busy teachers. Others who experienced dissatisfaction
in their own education feel that if they register a complaint to the
school, their child may suffer some discriminatory action. A number
feel impotent to effect change in any aspect of life and doubt whether
the school would solicit their judgment in an other than perfunctory
way. Finally, there are those who maintain a supportive school attitude but whose behavior is an illogical concomitant. With good
intent, they employ prodding, threat, physical punishment, and other
negative measures in the name of education. Each of these views is
unfortunate in that positive home-school relations are curtailed and
child growth and development adversely affected.

One might hope the reciprocal teacher view of slum homes would
promote greater cohesion between the two institutions. This is seldom true, as inner-city personnel often report they are blamed for
events fostered in the home, subjected to unfair and unreasoning
criticism, and confronted with apathy on every hand. A frequent
complaint is: "I can't do a thing with indifferent parents—they seem
to lack feeling and concern. I am not sure they care about anything."
But just as parents can be deceived about school objectives, so we
as teachers can misread behavior. It may be that a feeling of helpless-
ness in the face of family difficulty may underlie some of what looks
like unconcern. This is a defensive reaction, for one cannot remain in
a state of constant fear and remain well. In his account of life alone
in the Antarctic, Admiral Byrd described a situation uncommon to
him but too common among slumdwellers: "The tolerable quality of
a troublesome and dangerous existence is the fact that the mind
cannot remain continuously sensitive to anything. Repetitious dulling
impact sees to that." (6)

The opposing attitudes of parents and teachers are probably
created by the same cause—unfortunate experience of some, compounded by rumor and adopted by many. Nevertheless, where home
and school feel vulnerable to each other, hostility is apt to ensue with
each experiencing doubt and uncertainty regarding its proper role.
That improving information and increasing contact is the only useful
prescription could well be challenged by Paul Bowman (7), who,
after conducting a two-week summer session designed for teachers
and parents, observed that by the beginning of the second week

parents were complaining that the educators spoke a language all their own, were not interested in parents, engaged in clique behavior and appeared more involved in developing curriculum than children. The teachers who indicated no common interests with the parents dismissed all claims by the latter as overcritical. An open hostility followed which was never bridged—and this occurred in a group selected because of their interest in better understanding between home and school.

The problem appears to center about role misinterpretation and communication. In the absence of commonly understood, specific societal expectations, both home and school jealously guard certain functions while assuming different tasks to be within the other's province. Seldom are the assumed responsibilities conjunctive, so that failure is always considered the fault of the other party; advice is considered an imposition, always objectionable since it is given for matters outside one's responsibility; the common attitude is: "You mind your business, we mind ours." While devotion to duty may be unswerving, delineation of duty is unclear.

Certainly the initiative for action in resolving this conflict lies with the organized group, the community institution, the school. Responsibilities incumbent upon teachers extend beyond developing the mind, talent and person of their students and include offering guidance to the home in order that parents may reinforce and support educational programs. This involves sharing information with the home, organizing easy routes of communication and interpreting societal expectations.

If schools systematically sought from every parent his store of information about the pupil—his goals, friends, fears, strengths and weaknesses—classroom learning might proceed more efficiently. Then too, were teachers to communicate to parents whatever meaningful information they had about youngsters, more homes could improve the quality of their role. To foster this continuing two-way exchange, the school needs to organize definite and easy routes of communication. This is at once an attitudinal and a mechanical problem, for parents must be convinced that their communication is desired, and time, place and means must be understood. Since many parents work, they should know what kinds of problems may be handled by telephone, how and when to reach the instructor. When there are problems with the teacher which they feel cannot be discussed with her, parents should know the name and telephone number of some other person in the school who might help.

If unrealistic expectations of the home are engendered in the local school program, educators cannot hope to gain an audience for their interpretation of societal demands. Certainly there can be no request that youngsters be given two or three hours of absolute quiet for study each evening at home. Usually, circumstance precludes the likelihood of extended privacy; furthermore, without training in how to utilize solitude, slum children are not apt to succeed. It is better that the school provide a place on its premises if evening study is required. The request that children be exposed to more books in the home is also irrelevant, as finance if not choice disallows a household library. Again, the school might donate books if the need is actual. Help on homework is untenable for often children are more advanced than their parents. If the adult in the home is frequently subjected to the embarrassment of being expected to counsel and give direction on matters for which he lacks ability, frustration and alienation are likely to ensue. Only when the expectations of the local school are in order will parents listen to societal expectations. It follows that all expectations must be within the province of possibility.

Certain societal expectations are incumbent upon all, whether rich or poor, residing in slum or suburb. All parents have the responsibility to send their children to school interested and ready to learn. The best preparation involves developing curiosity or what is called a questing approach. While a child observes an event or experiences something new, he can be aided by responding to his queries with other questions rather than the customary "Because I said so," or "I don't know." Curiosity is the basis of learning; contrary to the opinion of some, a wealth of experiences are available within the central city to help parents foster this valuable mental stimulant. In Chicago, the Center for Urban Children is establishing a program to prepare mothers of low-income homes to teach their preschoolers basic cognitive skills needed for first grade.

Another societal expectation is that all parents will encourage pupil progress. Though the importance of motivational factors has repeatedly been demonstrated in studies where persons of similar intelligence exhibit wide differences in performance, only recently have we come to recognize the strong relationship between academic achievement and the self-concept children have of their own ability.

At Michigan State University, researchers found that as self-concept of ability is altered, there tend to be corresponding changes in grades achieved. What makes this relevant to the present discussion is that in attempts to change pupil self-concept by (a) formal learning groups and information sessions, (b) group and individual counseling, and (c) training parents to promote the improvement of child self view, only the last method resulted in a significant change as shown by improved grades (8). These findings indicating the importance of parental influence on self-concept seem to suggest that schools might well train parents how best to develop positive self-image at home. Meetings of parents and teachers with this objective would be more meaningful than social visits to the classroom once a year.

Pupil self-concept and confidence can be enhanced by parents who, in using guidance and encouragement, foster their child's successful completion of tasks without driving him or removing his freedom to fail. The freedom to fail, essential as it is to developing confidence, growth and success, is lost when parents consistently step in to complete a youngster's task. This often occurs in slum homes where the expediency of finishing an activity results in an older family member's completing what the young have set out to do. For the parent, impatience and the necessity to hurry allows no time to teach; for the child, no time to deliberate, to complete one's tasks, means no time to learn.

Where a realistic concept of self is not fostered, the result is discouraging. Some children become over-strivers and announce goals far beyond their past attainment. They are uncertain about what they can really expect of themselves. They cannot admit inadequacy or distinguish the reasonable from the unreasonable. Lacking confidence, they reduce their anxiety by aiming beyond what they can hope to achieve. It is as though they were saying, "My attainments aren't much but at least my goals are worthy of praise." And failure to reach lofty goals hardly counts as failing. Thus, if they succeed, their pleasure is great; if they fail, their self-respect does not suffer. Not knowing what they can do or how others will regard them necessarily implies a lack of self-respect (9).

It is important to recognize that goal setting and self-concept are inextricably related. A steady but realistic raising of aims is usual among self-confident children who are assured in their performance.

They may show pleasure and strong effort, but in a realistic fashion which places socially and self-approved limits on their achievement. They are not ashamed of poor performance on material which is clearly too difficult for them. On the other hand, they do not gloat over good performance on easy material. In contrast, the over-striver lacks a clear self-concept and hence is insecure, apprehensive, and inflexible. Those who withdraw appear self-conscious, dissatisfied with themselves, and anxious to take an easy way out. It is interesting to note that the assured pupil strives in response to criticism, whereas the worried, sensitive pupil seems to respond better to praise (10).

Finally, parents are expected by society to ensure their youngster's graduation from secondary school. Under no circumstance should the future of a boy or girl be sacrificed because of family financial need. Rather, parents might solicit temporary help from the school in securing a part-time job for their child. In cases where parents unsuccessfully seek employment for themselves, the school through its contacts is sometimes able to locate suitable positions. Certainly there should be no capitulation to the untenable proposal of some educators that we adopt a measure employed in parts of Europe to sustain pupil attendance; namely, that society pay the home.

Dropout problems in Europe are averted because of built-in circumstances or measures which our nation would find dubious or impossible to duplicate. Those who advocate monetary incentives to increase the holding power of slum schools point to countries such as Belgium and East Germany where leaving rates have declined ostensibly because of remunerative practices. In Belgium, parents are given stipend rewards in the form of family allowance for their children as long as the young remain in school. Scholarship grants, also paid to the parent, are available, increasing in value as the child advances through the grades. One might question whether this procedure does not in fact dislocate motivation for school attendance from the student to the parent, with the consequence that although the dropout rate is diminished, those who continue to attend may not necessarily be advancing.

In East Germany, students receive scholarship grants which are paid directly to them rather than to their parents. The stated objective of this procedure is that students should be able to enjoy the pleasant things of life to nearly the same extent as their employed peers and should not be tempted to leave school for the joy of motor scooters or gramophones. In addition, honor grades bring the scholar increased stipends. Ostensibly this is to stimulate intellectual development, but perhaps more important it serves to weaken family ties by relocating the economic dependency of the child from his parents to the state, thereby fostering greater allegiance to the state than the family (11).

Our country cannot afford to destroy its basic institution, the family, nor can we forfeit that strength of our nation which is shaped in the school. Progress lies not in a retreat to lesser ideals but in the enrichment of what is already ours. Home-school relations can and will improve—without payola.

COMMUNITY DEVELOPMENT

One of the most important aspects of inner-city education involves long-range development of the community. The need for action is implicit in one slumdweller's description of his neighborhood: "The more it [the slum] changes, the more it is the same." Though new faces and families arrive daily, charged with purpose and intent, the level of slum life remains constant, depressing, immutable. The last vestige of community seems to have disappeared as no formal protests are lodged from within against noisy and cluttered sidewalks, all-night cabarets, and disorderly hotels. Naturally vice flourishes under these conditions and transportation makes the locale accessible from all parts of the city. Nonresidents looking for illegal or illicit activity are able to get out from under the restraining mores of their own communities into the slum areas where there are neither restraints nor mobilized public opinions.

A climate favorable to change in communal attitude and behavior involves neighborhood identity. In the slum there is no natural neighborhood for many to identify with—only endless unplanned blocks, too much traffic, too many taverns, too few play areas, and no open space. Were order or attraction a part of the physical environment, one might reasonably expect some cause for identity. This is seldom the case. As the lack of neighborhood structure in the slum precludes any identification or allegiance by its membership, so it fails to influence in a positive way any internal improvement. In other words, what could be the most vital force, neighborhood identity, is the most impotent.

Moreover, daily experience acts to diminish prospects of activating aspiration, effort, identification—the personal elements requisite to fostering communal development. Often at the mercy of events, poor people lack money, contacts, and attitudes that might bend circumstance in their favor. Adversely affected by innovation and unable to effect change, the slumdweller's situation fosters a perception of self that leads to pessimism, passivity, and dissatisfaction; a cynicism about people and organizations; a syndrome of attitudes supporting only lethargy, despair, and indifference. The poor, believing their societal rank to carry no weight whatsoever, seldom congregate into organized bodies.

The school is the only institution that can give slumdwellers the self-concept and competence needed to bring about communal development. Any attempt to persuade these persons that their judgments can influence the direction of events will fail unless decisions are committed to such a course. To the extent that poor families try to improve the school, try to move events themselves and find they are ignored, their cynical view of educators will be reconfirmed, their fatalism and mistrust revived. If, however, by involvement in school affairs, parents can come to feel a sense of dignity, an awareness that their feelings count, that sensible judgments held by an organized body can carry influence, progress will be forthcoming. The experience gained in working with school groups can extend to the neighborhood, alter life in the street and lessen vice and disorder. That attitudes can be rehabilitated and environment mastered by neighborhood morale has already been demonstrated in deprived sections of Baltimore, Chicago, Miami, and New Orleans.

This transition to responsible citizenship through positive identity affects the young also. The troubled young people who create serious social difficulties today are for the most part those who have been unable to identify themselves with individuals or groups whose ideals and actions are consistent with a strong, decent social order. The full power of degrading influences within the slum is neither appreciated nor understood. We cannot expect young people to adopt standards of taste and behavior consistently higher than those of the adults who are their models. Our real task as educators, therefore, is to create satisfactory channels of communication within the community so that young boys and girls may come into contact with older people of integrity who may serve as worthy models. The energy and nature of youth demand a cause—better they should be committed to growth than destruction, law than disorder (12).

Lacking a large identity, the block dweller of the slum feels out of place elsewhere. But in the future he must become a city dweller. This will not occur by moving him, sweeping away his security, or tearing down the neighborhood in which he resides. It will transpire through a rehabilitation of attitudes, an alteration of self-concepts, and the advancement of an ever-enlarging identity with neighborhood, borough, city and nation. If our society is defeated in the war against poverty, it will not be by our prospect but by our perspective. Better that we be optimistic than give pessimism the label of realism.

RESOURCES

(1)   Hess, Robert D., "Maternal Teaching Styles and Educational Retardation," in *Mental Health and Achievement,* eds. E. Paul Torrance and Robert D. Strom (New York: John Wiley & Sons, 1965), Chap. II.

(2)   McCarthy, Dorothea, "Language Development in Children," in *Manual of Child Psychology,* ed. Leonard Carmichael (New York: John Wiley & Sons, 1954), pp. 584–86.

(3)   Strom, Robert D., *The Tragic Migration* (Washington, D.C.: the Department of Home Economics, National Education Association, 1964), pp. 6–8, 13.

(4)   Educational Policies Commission of the National Education Association, *Education and the Disadvantaged American* (Washington, D.C., 1962), p. 27.

(5)   Abbott, Mary K., "The Culturally Handicapped Student and the Reading Process" (San Francisco: Public Schools Community Improvement Project, 1964), p. 2, mimeographed.

(6)   Byrd, Richard E., *Alone* (New York: G. P. Putnam Sons, 1938), p. 86.

(7) Bowman, Paul H., "Family Role in the Mental Health of School Children," in *Mental Health and Achievement,* eds. E. Paul Torrance and Robert D. Strom (New York: John Wiley & Sons, 1965), Chap. I.

(8) Brookover, W., T. Shaler, and A. Paterson, "Self-Concept of Ability and School Achievement," *Sociology of Education,* Vol. 37 (Spring 1964), pp. 271–78.

(9) Cronbach, Lee J., *Educational Psychology,* second edition (New York: Harcourt, Brace and World, Inc., 1963), pp. 466–573.

(10) Strom, Robert D., "Raising Aspirations of Youth," *Catholic Education Review,* Vol. LXII (May 1964), pp. 289–97.

(11) Strom, Robert D., "How Europeans Face Up to Their Dropout Problem," *The Clearing House,* Vol. 38, No. 7 (March 1964), pp. 431–33.

(12) Farnsworth, Dana L., "Motivation for Learning," *Rhode Island College Journal,* Vol. 1, No. 2 (March 1960), pp. 55–64.

Preparation and Recruitment of Teachers

3

Teachers in the slum are more often subjected to undue criticism and censure than their rural and suburban counterparts. The vast army of out-of-school unemployed dropouts is seen as evidence of past failure in slum education; rising crime rates and increasing juvenile disorder are viewed as indications of current failure. That inner-city classrooms are overcrowded, high rates of mobility and truancy obtain, numerous learning difficulties are sustained and familial cooperation is not forthcoming—these factors are considered not precipitating but attendant problems, unrelated to effective instruction. *Nevertheless, some of the finest teaching in this country is being done by dedicated instructors who choose to work among the disadvantaged.*

STAFFING THE DIFFICULT SCHOOLS

Ordinarily the task of staffing so-called difficult schools is perplexing, as new personnel, if given the option, seldom choose a position in low-income neighborhoods. Overwhelmed by the prospect of confronting divergent social-behavioral norms and a large number of atypical children with special learning problems, candidates imagine a type of blackboard jungle in which the major classroom function is maintenance of discipline. Some beginners in education feel that prospective working conditions lack elements vital to their satisfaction and morale, such as small classes, an attractive building and ample free periods. An absence of status, recognition and esteem complete the dreary outlook. In polite rejection, a few teachers cite the inaccessibility of the school, or want of transportation, as the decisive deterrent. Little wonder that in spite of intensive recruitment efforts, not a single large city from coast to coast has been able to adequately staff the schools in its disadvantaged areas.

While a number of recruitment schemes have been devised to fill inner-city vacancies, the most prominent method seems to be the arbitrary assignment of new and inexperienced teachers. As Harry Rivlin, dean of teacher education for the City University of New York, has pointed out, "Teaching differs from every other profession in that it is the only one in which the most complex and most difficult problems are assigned to the least expert and least experienced practitioners." However, the procedure of involuntary assignment is not always agreed upon. For example, 34 out of 100 teachers appointed to the borough of Manhattan do not accept appointments in the schools to which they have been assigned (1). Many of those who reluctantly comply with the administrative request remain in the slum school only long enough to secure tenure or a transfer to a site of more favored economic circumstance. Thus it is not strange that the recent Hauser study of education in Chicago found inner-city schools to be more overcrowded; employing less experienced, less educated teachers; and sustaining a higher incidence of temporary appointments among staff members and a higher rate of faculty turnover than schools in outlying areas (2).

Arbitrary assignment is not the only possible method of recruiting for the slum schools. Other measures that have been suggested include rotation of personnel, establishment of educational parks or plazas and programs designed to develop indigenous leadership. John Galbraith, Harvard University economist, has recently proposed to ameliorate the situation by creating a national teaching corps composed of 10,000 of the nation's best educators. These persons would be paid $12,000 per annum to work in the urban and rural schools where urgent efforts are needed (3). None of the foregoing proposals appear likely to receive wide support.

COLLEGIATE TRAINING

There is a more important problem than mere recruitment. High rates of staff turnover in slum schools in nearly every urban complex lend credence to the assertion that a more adequate type of training is needed by those assigned to such institutions. This is not because teaching is poor compared with the past but because the demands of the present and future are so high. There are indigenous to slum school assignments certain difficulties which require special training for the teacher. Yet, unlike the social worker and other members of the supportive staff who are trained in urban sociology, teachers often lack knowledge which might increase the relevance of instruction, the length of their tenure and the degree of their satisfaction.

Teacher training institutions purporting to equip candidates for positions in almost any type of environment must begin to provide more than cursory attention to whatever tasks, difficulties and procedures which appear vital to successful teaching in poor neighborhoods. This responsibility does not pertain exclusively to the urban university or college but is incumbent upon all institutions where future teachers are being prepared, for the population mobility in our nation includes its teachers. Untrained to teach in the big city, those educated elsewhere are not promising recruits when because of marriage or other reasons their circumstance brings them to an urban residence. We cannot change facts by ignoring them and the fact is that we live in an era when about 80 percent of our population will reside in urban centers. A striking example is in the cities of California where 1,700 new residents arrive daily. The implication for teacher training should be obvious.

URBAN SOCIOLOGY AND INSTRUCTION

The term *readiness* is as applicable to teachers as it is to students. Unless one is prepared for a position in the slum context, each school day is likely to end in emotional exhaustion. This effete condition is a common complaint among the young and inexperienced whose first assignment involves an inner-city classroom. Newcomers to the profession naturally tend to gauge the extent of their effectiveness by visible pupil progress. When positive results are not forthcoming, ego defenses are activated and, in a needless effort to defend self, the instructor projects a cloud of failure onto the student. Perhaps we facilitate this manner of reasoning by describing low-income children with adjectives like *underprivileged, handicapped, culturally deprived,* and *disadvantaged.* Although the referent is their environmental limitation, the terms tend to create an image of less potential. John Niemeyer, president of Bank Street College in New York City, contends, "A major reason for low achievement among children in poor neighborhoods is the low expectation as to their learning capacity held

lack of urban training for teachers

aching and guidance are forfeited because regarding the customs, mores, and values that govern behavior, the mechanisms through which slum children can most be influenced; the structure and operation of powerful peer groups; the indigenous system of incentives that affect motivation and discipline; the educational strengths emerging from life in an extended family; the real causes underlying academic difficulty; the potential support for elements of education in the home; and the manner and media for communication with parents. Although most prospective teachers need and desire training in these areas, seldom do college counseling, curriculum and scheduling encourage it. Were the future teachers in any academic major to receive some training in urban sociology, psychology of motivation, culture pattern and personality, human development and the teaching of reading, our circumstance within the slum might be markedly improved in terms of instructional quality, pupil progress, home-school relations, and teacher morale and tenure.

From urban sociology, one can gain insight about the positive features emerging from life in the extended family. Hopefully these factors might be given consideration in the organization and conduct of classroom instruction. When educators fail to use the potential academic strengths of childhood experience in low-income groups, such strengths become nonfunctional. Much of the slum youngster's competitive potential vanishes when he is forced to compete by using strengths not engendered in his background but characteristic of life in middle-class families. Even a cursory comparison of differences in family strengths at low- and middle-income levels is sufficient to reveal that our problem is not so much whether school expectations in the slum are too high or too low as whether they are inappropriate.

The dominant theme which pervades the growth of children in small middle-class families is planning. Often their birth, rearing, school objectives and career preparation are planned. Motivated largely by hopes for the future of child members, these families emphasize cooperative relations and planning with the young. Democratic expression is accompanied by an individualization of roles and activities for each member of the family. This makes for an individual emphasis in development and thinking as well. The family members are noncompeting, with father, mother and children all going their own ways.

Abstaining from competition within, the small middle-income family assumes what Margaret Mead (5) calls the sidewise look, meaning that parents compare and measure their children primarily with neighboring youngsters, members of the same social class or school. As the parents do so much for them, the children are expected to do a great deal in return. The pressure for achievement and social advance is constant. Because of the small number of children, parents allow no margin of error or failure.

These youngsters are readily able to meet most of the school's expectations. It is not difficult for them to plan with the teacher for both proximate and ultimate objectives. Home life has given them a base for decision making. They understand and accept the concepts of scheduling, time and order—when tasks and assignments are to be completed. Effective study habits pose no problem as both their experience and home environment are supportive of solitary pursuits. The fact that most schoolwork entails individual assignments involves no adjustment or adaptation since they are used to working alone. The freedom of their homes has given impetus to the creative thinking processes as well as to aspects of self-discipline. The system of competition with others is in accord with their value structure and incentive base. In short, such children are likely to fit into the school establishment.

On the other hand, the extended low-income family, usually unplanned in number, supports a group orientation rather than the individual emphasis of small families. From childhood on, the young of large households play together, with play confined ordinarily to the sibling group. Then too, children work together as a team, often undertaking some responsibilities assumed by parents in smaller homes. As crises and problems arise, group cohesion is evidenced by the device of sticking together to surmount difficulty. Children tend to develop an ability to absorb frequent minor crises, since the strain is shared.

There is little opportunity for making decisions because what one is able to do depends on what others are doing. Circumstance and the behavior of others are the factors that determine what one can or cannot do. Little is left to choice, from the hand-me-down garment to the use of a room by oneself.

With large family living go emphases on qualities of behavior that will benefit the group before the individual. Conformity is valued above self-expression, listening above talking, cooperation above individual effort. The necessity to function as a unit allows little comparison wtih neighbor children. A greater value is attached to duty than achievement; quitting school to help with family finance may be viewed in greater favor than remaining to graduate. Life is governed more by rule than principle and misbehavior is treated not by cause or intent but subject to standard punishment for a given act.

The multiplicity of relationships in a large family obviously form the potential for an easy transition into group learning situations. Often these youngsters have developed many requisites to successful participation in group work, as they appear cooperative, able to share, tolerant, willing to accept others and many are unselfish. However, they quickly find the school is geared to individual pursuits. Often they will do poorly in study habits since they lack a place at home and training in the use of solitude and concentration. Their experiences with crowding and lack of privacy have curtailed the development of individuality and self-sufficiency. Unlike the middle-class child from a small family whose background is in accord with school expectations of individual work, children from the large low-income family must adjust and adapt their learning style. The question whether there is a relation between size of family group in which a person is reared and size of classroom working group in which he makes the best adjustment is unanswered. However, in studying adjustment to occupational work groups, James Bossard (6) found that persons reared in small families are happiest in jobs where they work alone or with one other person. Similarly, persons reared in large families make better occupational adjustments when working in large groups.

Pupils from extended families in the slum are often unfamiliar with scheduling, time limits, and assignment deadlines. In the absence of planning at home and with little background in making decisions, they find themselves in difficulty when confronted with deliberative situations in which circumstance does not choose for them but rather they themselves must decide alone. They tend to find multiple choice examinations much more difficult than true-false. Nevertheless, these children have a remarkable degree of independence and seldom need continual adult approval for their actions. As a result, they might well be given responsibilities in the classroom; but under the current system, anyone with poor grades is denied such an opportunity. Their home exposure to conformity might tend to retard creativity and induce the viewpoint that school as an institution demands physical behavior rather than mental processes. Finally, the incentive system of working against others is unlikely to motivate such children and neither will failure bring a zealous search for knowledge. It appears that we must use whatever familial strengths are engendered in the low-income home to help the child become an effective learner. Better that we modify our expectations than presume he can alter his needs. Ostensibly our schools are flexible in their strength: ought we not then to utilize the prospects poor youngsters bring to their classrooms?

DISCIPLINE IN THE CLASSROOM

Teacher candidates express more apprehension about discipline than any other aspect of instruction. That even educators of some experience feel this concern is shown in a recent study of 78 elementary teachers who indicate discipline to be their major classroom difficulty (7). Usually pupil misbehavior is confined to interruption or inconvenience, although frustration and failure are sometimes produced. Up to now, restraint of physical violence has rarely been necessary, but recent reports from New York City, Detroit and Chicago indicate that roughhouse behavior is increasing in our large cities. Pupil attacks on teachers have prompted some metropolitan centers to station policemen in troublesome schools in order to deter or repress further incidents (8). In the slums especially, the problem of discipline is actual.

In spite of the fact that prospective elementary and high school instructors may expect to encounter instances of misconduct and class disorder, most of them will not receive any practical instruction at college in handling such matters. Two basic reasons appear to cause the professorial conspiracy of silence on this subject. Some believe that discipline problems arise only in response to unfair treatment, that there are no culpably misbehaving children but only unsympathetic and punitive teachers. This doctrine is usually embraced by those whose teaching has been confined to higher education, where one seldom, if ever, must cope with unacceptable behavior. Others believe that the lessons of rapport and discipline are inextricably linked and therefore can only be learned by trial and error, by experience. Unfortunately, although experience may be the best teacher, it is also the toughest, as one often gets the test first and the lesson afterward. Sometimes there is no lesson, sometimes the lesson comes too late. Perhaps Tom Sawyer said it best (9):

> And he cleared out with the hundred camels, and left that man to wander around poor and miserable and friendless the rest of his days in the Desert.
>
> Jim said he'd bet it was a lesson to him.
>
> "Yes," Tom says, "and like a considerable many lessons a body gets. They ain't no account, because the thing don't ever happen the same way again—and can't. The time Hen Scovil fell down the chimbly and cripples his back for life, everybody said it would be a lesson to him. What kind of a lesson? How was he going to use it? He couldn't climb chimblies no more, and he hadn't no more backs to break."
>
> "All de same, Mars Tom, dey is sech a thing as learnin' by expe'ence. De Good Book say de burnt chile shun de fire."
>
> "Well, I ain't denying that a thing's a lesson if it's a thing that can happen twice just the same way. There's lots of such things, and they educate a person, that's what Uncle Abner always said; but there's forty million lots of the other kind—the kind that don't happen the same way twice—and they ain't no real use, they ain't no more instructive than the smallpox. When you've got it, it ain't no good to find out you ought to been vaccinated, and it ain't no good to get vaccinated afterward, because the smallpox don't come but once. But, on the other hand, Uncle Abner said a person that had took a bull by the tail once had

learned sixty or seventy times as much as a person that hadn't, and said a person that started to carry a cat home by the tail was getting knowledge that was always going to be useful to him. But I can tell you, Jim, Uncle Abner was down on them people that's all the time trying to dig a lesson out of everything that happens, no matter whether . . ."

But Jim was asleep. Tom looked kind of ashamed, because you know a person always feels bad when he is talking uncommon fine and thinks the other person is admiring, and the other person goes to sleep that way.*

Ordinarily new personnel are assigned to a master teacher, someone they can turn to for support and encouragement, guidance and advice. However, the high incidence of staff turnover in slum schools means that there are fewer master teachers, a lower proportion of experienced personnel. Apart from weakening faculty cohesion, this situation limits the prospect of a new teacher for receiving needed assistance. When there is no access to helpful supervision, inappropriate methods of classroom operation are bound to be perpetuated, to the disadvantage of both teacher and pupil (10).

Without counsel, the new instructor may not know the hazards of using embarrassment, ridicule, or sarcasm as measures of control. With good intent, one may hope to correct behavior by employing statements like "Don't act like a kindergartener. Do you want to move to your little sister's room?" Granted, immediate compliance may follow, but this method can undermine positive teacher-pupil rapport in the future. Similarly, indiscriminate punishment of an entire class until we find out "who did it" is unwise. This is not just because tattling or informing are infrequent in the slum but because innocent bystanders may decide that if they are going to be punished anyway, there is no point in trying to obey the rules. Just as public reprimanding of an individual can have severe repercussions, so too can an inadvertent mixture of discipline and academic penalty. To motivate class members by asserting that "No one will go to recess until everyone is done with the assignment" places a tremendous pressure on slow learners who are already having difficulty without the addition of peer disdain.

---

* From *Tom Sawyer Abroad and Other Stories,* by Samuel L. Clemens, pp. 85–87. Copyright 1928, Harper & Row, Publishers, Inc. Reprinted by permission.

Unless aware, the new teacher may regard all cases of misconduct as directed personally toward him. He may feel guilty for each act of disorder and disrespect in the classroom. We sometimes induce this guilt when we (those of us not in the public school classrooms) assume that problems would not arise in the first place if the teacher really deserved respect, treated the class fairly. Therefore, few newcomers approach their administrator for assistance or counsel regarding pupil misbehavior because to do so would be tantamount to admission of teacher failure. After an extended period of discontent and discouragement, some talented and potentially capable young teachers resign, while other less desirable persons who do not try to teach may remain in the classroom.

Many of us in higher education have been remiss in our obligation to adequately prepare teacher candidates to meet behavioral problems that might confront them upon assignment to an inner-city school. To be sure, discipline is more a matter of opinion than science. Yet the fact that discipline cannot be placed on a strictly scientific basis does not mean that one position is as good as another or that no instruction in the alternatives is warranted. Society is constantly called upon to resolve issues of greater moment with less objective evidence for decision making than we now have regarding discipline. Whether responsibility for instruction in this matter is to be considered the province of courses in human development, educational psychology, the psychology of motivation, adolescent psychology or group dynamics is of secondary importance. What is primary is that it be offered.

As the imposition of external standards and controls on individual conduct, discipline has always been considered an important aspect of child learning in every part of the world. In this country discipline serves several functions. First, it is necessary for socialization—for learning the culturally approved and tolerated standards of conduct. Second, discipline is necessary for normal personality maturation—for acquiring aspects of adult behavior such as dependability, self-control, self-reliance, and tolerance of frustration. These traits do not occur spontaneously but only in response to sustained societal expectations and demands. Third, discipline is necessary for the internalization of moral standards and obligations or, in other words, the development of conscience. Finally, discipline is necessary for the emotional security of the young. Without the guidance provided by clearly defined limitations and controls, too great a burden is placed upon a child's limited capacity for self-control. He may thus become bewildered and apprehensive (11).

Agreement on the need for discipline is not always accompanied by a consensus as to method. This is as it should be because no method of discipline is equally effective with all children. Indeed, differences in pupil response to varying measures of classroom control are as diverse as individual differences in terms of ability, even though we are more aware of the latter.

Age and sex are also important variables for consideration. Younger children have more limited controls and less well developed concepts of right and wrong; older youngsters can better accept limitations and postpone immediate gratification. Girls may be expected to exhibit more emotional upset than boys, although they create disorders of a less hostile and destructive nature.

Social class is also a factor in determination of disciplinary method and effect. In neighborhoods of low income where parents often resort to harsh discipline and physical punishment, careful supervision of children is rare. Crowded living conditions usually mean that the young slum child is free to run unsupervised in the streets and alleys of his locale at an age when the suburban youngster is limited to his own yard. Consequently, during the early formative years, low-income families yield to the peer group much of their influence. Not only are peer groups formed earlier in the slum than in the suburb but their cohesion is stronger since they serve more as family substitute than as an extra group for affinity and identification. Even in the home, adjustment of behavior is made more to peers than to adults, as older children become responsible for the discipline of smaller siblings.

Powerful peer influences extend to affect pupil-teacher rapport and classroom behavior. With few if any illusions about adult omniscience, even the most youthful of slum children are easily dissuaded by their fellows from accepting the teacher's authority, seeking his approval, or establishing any positive relationships with the educational institution. The school's offer of social recognition, ultimate earning power, and vocational satisfaction presents little in the way of current primary status for a child whose peers place no value on learning or its outcomes.

Apparently the social values of low-income peer groups must be known if we are to use discipline that is primarily preventive of misconduct, secondarily corrective and never retributive. The effectiveness of disciplinary method will depend upon its compatability with the operant value system. For example, if an individual is caught cheating, it is germane to know whether and to what extent cheating is accepted, tolerated, or disapproved by his peer group. We now have rather simple instruments by which this information can be gathered (12). In the final analysis, a teacher's effectiveness is adversely affected if his understanding of student behavioral norms is not in direct relation to reality. It follows that to know the student better is to be a better teacher.

THE URBAN SPECIALIST

Knowing the slum and its children is important, but something more is needed to provide student advance. Many pupils from neighborhoods of low income are markedly retarded in fundamental academic subjects. George Spache, head of the reading laboratory at Florida University, contends that of the youngsters entering junior high school in some urban districts, as many as 30 percent may not have developed the reading comprehension skills needed to do schoolwork on that level. Moreover, Francis Keppel, U.S. Commissioner of Education, has reported that one third of the high school English teachers in this country did not major in English, that they do not consider themselves well prepared to teach oral and composition skills, and that 90 percent of them do not think they are well prepared for teaching reading (13). To recommend that every candidate for the profession, regardless of academic interest, be schooled in the teaching of reading within his field can be helpful, as is demonstrated by gratifying results at Philadelphia's Edison High School (14).

However, the need is not confined to reading alone. In mathematics, for instance, where learning difficulties are cumulative, more than one third of all seventh-grade classes are taught by teachers with less than two general courses in college mathematics (15). We are coming to recognize that teachers who are most effective know the elements of their subject well. By *superior training* is not meant exposure to a profusion of mathematics courses for the prospective mathematics teacher, but rather an emphasis on the parts of math which he will teach. A prospective teacher of elementary mathematics may gain more insight by studying elementary mathematics from an advanced point of view than by studying, say, differential equations or modern algebra (16). The more fruitful task, in reading and mathematics especially, appears to be an emphasis on remedial instruction and diagnostics, on determining not how poor a pupil is but what difficulties preclude his success. If we persist in emphasizing only a pupil's product—that is to say, his answers and performance—rather than the processes he employs to derive answers, it is unlikely that the difficulties of learning will be determined or resolved. Teacher experience in the slum strongly suggests an increase in remedial and diagnostic training in the view of prevailing needs.

In order to bridge the gap that separates the home and school, to diminish the social distance between parent and teacher, training in human relations is being considered. Poor families cannot initially be expected to gain enthusiasm or insight through lectures, organized meetings, or other formal activities that might demand unrealistic levels of scholarship and concentration. Instead they can be involved through visits to the home by their child's teacher, individual conferences at school, observation of classroom lessons and group discussions with other parents on problems related to child development. All of these types of meetings with parents can be more effectively used by teachers who are trained in conference techniques and procedures. Most instructors need help in conducting effective conferences and are frank to admit it. The Queens College study cited earlier on page 36 showed that teachers regard relations with parents as their second most difficult problem. Again, few candidates will receive any training in this area.

In response to the need for an ever increasing competence among teachers assigned to "difficult" schools, seventeen New York City colleges and universities are now cooperating with the City Board of Education to provide specially designed training courses. The institutions involved are Bank Street College, Brooklyn College, City College, Fordham University, Hunter College, Long Island University, Marymount Manhattan College, New York Medical College, New York University, Notre Dame College, Pratt Institute, Queens College, St. Johns University, St. Joseph's College, Teachers College of Columbia University, Wagner College and Yeshiva University. Each of these organizations conducts its individual program in campus schools established in 33 public elementary buildings most of which are located in low-income districts. Here student teachers, along with preservice candidates, observe and participate in demonstration lessons and classroom operation as well as gain firsthand information about community mores and behavior. The campus school arrangement also provides an opportunity for educators to try out new methods, techniques, and materials designed to meet the needs of disadvantaged children.

The fact that college professors conduct the demonstration lessons in these slum school projects is considered a healthy scheme in that members of higher education thus maintain closer contact with public school life than might otherwise be the case. Some view this framework as indicative of a move toward adoption of James Conant's proposed "clinical professorship." Conant has urged that every institution purporting to train teachers employ three or four clinical professors who, as competent scholars, spend at least half their time teaching in their particular discipline and the remaining portion supervising, counseling and conferring with student teachers as well as deciding on their certification (17). Needless to say, opinion is strong but split as to the advisability of the Conant proposal.

Although the foresight, planning, and zeal of New York City teacher training efforts is receiving wide commendation, those responsible for the program are quick to remind us that theirs is a limited effort—that much remains to be done. The number of teachers being prepared by these programs is far too small to meet current needs. Moreover, the size of the sample as well as the fact that teachers are voluntarily involved in these programs rather than arbitrarily assigned, as is usual, tends to distort the picture somewhat. Nevertheless, the innovation in leadership function alone can increase the province of such courses in other cities and, in so doing, enhance the chance of more children of the slum to gain a better education.

INSERVICE PROGRAMS

For most of the 150,000 teachers who graduate from college each year there will have been no access to a curriculum of specialized training for urban positions. Even were this alternative available, there is no certainty that large numbers of students would elect its pursuit. As in the past, so in the future, more slum classrooms will be filled by assignment by than by choice. Hopefully, some of the newcomers will have taken at least some preparatory work in urban sociology, but even this will not be the mode. Under the circumstance, a thorough system of inservice education seems warranted.

The importance of giving new teachers initial experiences that are satisfying cannot be overemphasized. Though many refuse to acknowledge it, the degree to which adjustment is satisfactory to the individual first-year teacher affects the quality of his service to the school, influences his decision to remain with the system, and may determine whether or not he continues in the profession (18). The best way to ensure satisfactory adjustment is through a comprehensive and effective orientation program. Though teachers are interested chiefly in matters of knowing the community, the school and its procedures, most orientation programs focus on minor administrative duties of teachers or introductions of other staff members and are seldom related to inservice development.

Because the necessary preparation for a slum classroom is so important, it would seem a worthwhile consideration to bring newly hired teachers assigned to the low-income district onto the job a month early. During the period before school opens, they can attend daily workshop sessions on understanding the community, human relations, classroom practices, the functions of the supportive staff, and what to do in any contingency. These meetings could be directed by the principal or by one of the supportive staff members, such as the social worker, the placement counselor, the psychologist, or the school nurse. Discussions, lectures, films and organized trips would be an integral part of the sessions. Giving this opportunity to the new teacher can mean the difference between success and failure in the classroom.

Most educators agree that new staff members must not be forgotten once they enter the classroom. Yet a study by the National Education Association Research Division on first-year teachers (19) shows that while 85 percent needed help in handling discipline problems, 52 percent received little or none; while 66 percent needed help in getting acquainted with the community, 62 percent received little or none; while 89 percent needed understanding about assistance from supportive staff like the social worker, school nurse and guidance counselor, 54 percent received little or none; while 93 percent needed help in keeping and making out official records and reports, 34 percent received little or none; while 83 percent needed help in working with retarded and gifted children, 73 percent received little or none;

while 85 percent needed help in understanding the goals of the school, 35 percent received little or none; while 78 percent needed help in making effective use of community resources, 72 percent received little or none. It is imperative that every new teacher entering the slum school be assigned a more experienced staff member to whom he can bring questions and problems. Where high turnover results in a small number of experienced personnel, each veteran may have to assume the responsibility for helping more than one newcomer. The administrator also should assist in this adjustment so that no artificial barriers are established between classroom and central office.

Programs of inservice training ought not to be predicated on the assumption that all teachers have the same needs or require the same instruction at the same time in the same way. When given a chance to select from several alternative courses, teachers usually choose aspects of learning in which they lack strength and desire improvement. The factor of time, like choice, also seems important for making inservice meetings worthwhile. An issue can receive no more than perfunctory attention when the interested parties gather only once a month for an after-school meeting. To set aside several entire days a year specifically for inservice training seems to be a more useful procedure. On these occasions instructors would attend the meetings concerning their particular interest.

One group might conceivably be interested in the improvement of classroom evaluation. These participants could study how to use informal testing techniques, including open-book examinations; how to identify potential in other than paper and pencil tests; or how to administer standardized tests. After emphasizing the importance of testing aspects such as drawing inferences, completing sentences, and following time limits and directions, training might include the techniques for meaningful drill in these skills. Gaining familiarity with practice materials designed to make children more sophisticated with reference to testing situations is also valuable. A discussion of the limitations of group verbal I.Q. tests for disadvantaged children and the diminishing I.Q. phenomenon can be followed with helps on administering and interpreting nonverbal examinations as measures of potential.

Other teachers are interested in pursuing such topics as techniques in improving the self-image of children, remedial instruction and materials for minority groups, conferring with and reporting to parents, and understanding the peer group. Because of the pressure for educating children at an earlier age, some elementary teachers might wish to have a refresher course regarding the development of preschool children. Then too, upper elementary grade teachers who have taken child psychology can be baffled as to handling the problem of students who are overaged for their grade level. Using knowledgeable instructors to lead these sessions can result in a helpful and satisfying experience for all staff members. It is well to remind ourselves that the reversal from deprivation to dignity in the slum depends in great measure on the school. Only with prepared teachers can we offer young people a readiness for the future.

RESOURCES

(1)   Haubrich, Vernon F., "Teachers for Big City Schools," in *Education in Depressed Areas,* ed. A. Harry Passow (New York: Teachers College, Columbia University, 1963), p. 246.

(2)   National School Public Relations Association, *Education USA* (Washington, D.C.: the Association, a Department of the National Education Association, April 9, 1964), pp. 125–29.

(3)   Galbraith, John Kenneth, "A Two-Part Answer to Poverty," *U.S. News and World Report,* Vol. 56 (June 22, 1964), pp. 57–58.

(4)   Strom, Robert D., "The School Dropout and the Family," *School and Society,* Vol. 92, No. 2243 (April 1964), pp. 191–92.

(5)   Mead, Margaret, *And Keep Your Powder Dry* (New York: William Morrow and Co., 1943), p. 109.

(6)   Bossard, James H. S., and Eleanor S. Bell, *The Large Family System* (Philadelphia: University of Pennsylvania Press, 1956), pp. 126–47.

(7)   National School Public Relations Association, *Trends in School Public Relations* (Washington, D.C.: the Association, a Department of the National Education Association, April 15, 1964), p. 3.

(8)   National School Public Relations Association, *Education USA* (Washington, D.C.: the Association, a Department of the National Education Association, March 12, 1964), p. 109.

(9)   Clemens, Samuel L., *Tom Sawyer Abroad and Other Stories* (New York: Harper & Row, Publishers, Inc., 1928), pp. 85–87.

(10)   Openshaw, M. Karl, "Chicago," in *The Development of the Career Teacher: Professional Responsibility for Continuing Education* (Washington, D.C.: National Commission on Teacher Education and Professional Standards, National Education Association, 1964), p. 41.

(11)   Ausubel, David P., "A New Look at Classroom Discipline," *Phi Delta Kappan*, Vol. 43 (October 1961), pp. 25–30.

(12)   Strom, Robert D., "Comparison of Adolescent and Adult Behavioral Norm Properties," *Journal of Educational Psychology*, Vol. 54, No. 6 (December 1963), pp. 322–30.

(13)   National School Public Relations Association, *Education USA* (Washington, D.C.: the Association, a Department of the National Education Association, Feb. 6, 1964), p. 89.

(14)   Clark, Robert Wayne, "Summary Report: Language Arts Improvement Project for Edison High School" (Philadelphia: Public Schools, August 1, 1963), 7 pp., mimeographed.

(15)   *The New York Times*, September 15, 1963, Sec. 7, p. 1 ("It's Teacher's Turn in the Corner," Fred M. Hechinger's review of *The Education of American Teachers* by James Conant. New York: McGraw-Hill Book Company, 1963, 275 pp.).

(16)   Panel on Educational Research and Development for the President's Science Advisory Committee, *Innovation and Experiment in Education* (Washington, D.C.: Government Printing Office, March 1964), p. 23.

(17)   Conant, James B., *The Education of American Teachers* (New York: McGraw-Hill Book Company, 1963), 275 pp.

(18)   Strickler, Robert W., "Follow Through with the First-Year Teacher," *Educational Administration and Supervision*, Vol. 45 (January 1959), pp. 1–6.

(19)   National Education Association, Research Division, "First-Year Teachers in 1954–55," *National Education Association Research Bulletin*, No. 34 (February 1956), pp. 1–8.

A Supportive School Staff

4

Teachers daily encounter obstacles to classroom progress, barriers to pupil achievement. Nevertheless, the means by which many of these difficulties are resolved represents a vast improvement over the procedures of yesteryear. No longer is each instructor expected to assume exclusive responsibility for a given number of students, to provide an appropriate remedy for any and all problems that might arise among class members. Today the responsibility for pupil advance and well-being is shared by other professionals outside the classroom, trained specialists whose area of competence enables them to handle issues for which teachers are unprepared. Whether their backgrounds be in guidance or social work, nursing or remedial reading, psychology or library science, supervision or administration, each of these specialists has a single function: to help teachers and pupils.

In order that resource persons of differing talents may make their unique contribution to the education of children, staff relations must of necessity be characterized by cooperation, interdependence, and mutual effort. In the main, teachers recognize the value of a close rapport between themselves and other staff members who are equipped to offer assistance. But sometimes there is a wall that prevents an educator from utilizing services his colleagues stand ready to offer. For many the wall may be one of access, availability, the red tape to be gone through before receiving help. For some the wall may be built of misgivings, a lack of confidence in the outcomes of consultation. For others the wall may be structured of a personal reticence about soliciting help: they may believe that seeking assistance is tantamount to admitting failure. But by far the most common element basing the wall is unawareness of the important functions that a supportive staff can perform. To diminish walls wherever they exist, in both number and size, it is appropriate to examine some of the supportive staff roles in relation to the teacher, especially the ways in which the staff can help an instructor reach expectations and goals, share tasks and responsibilities, and improve working conditions.

GUIDANCE COUNSELOR

In the person of the school counselor, teachers have a valuable resource for helping children. However, like the other supportive specialists, guidance personnel represent a latent contribution unless activated by teacher referral. Hopefully, the counselor and teacher may act in concert, since they share mutual goals of facilitating pupil orientation, growth and direction. More specifically, a counselor can help the teacher by assisting in the planning of curriculum, increasing motivation, fostering pupil adjustment and self-understanding, determining remedial needs and diagnostic difficulties. To carry out these responsibilities, guidance personnel collect comprehensive significant information about each student, including scores on psychological, personality and achievement tests; results of social and emotional adjustment inventories; remarks on anecdotal and cumulative records. Because of his reliance upon objective data, the counselor is often misperceived by teachers as primarily a testing specialist, an evaluation expert. He is looked upon with reserve by those who share Pitirim Sorokin's view about the ubiquitous use of tests in our society:

> At the present time in the Western countries almost every individual is tested from the cradle to the grave, and before and

after every important event in his life. He is given a battery of tests after his birth, in his nursery school and kindergarten, in his elementary, high school, and college, before and after his draft into the armed forces, before and during his marriage, before and after his gainful employment, and so on, up to the tests preceding and following death. His life career is largely determined by these tests. Beginning with intelligence tests and ending with the tests of loyalty and subversity, various testers have replaced the old-fashioned angel-guardians that supposedly guided the life-course of each person. We are living in an age of testocracy. By their tests of our intelligence, emotional stability, character, aptitude, unconscious drives, and other characteristics of our personality, the testocrats largely decide our vocation and occupation. They play an important role in our promotions or demotions, successes and failures, in our social position, reputation, and influence. They determine our normality or abnormality, our superior intelligence or hopeless stupidity, our loyalty or subversity. By all this they are largely responsible for our happiness or despair and, finally, for our long life or premature death.* (1)

To be sure, the counselor administers many tests, making the results known to the principal and superintendent in order to determine needed emphases in different areas of instruction, to assess pupil progress from year to year, and to evaluate the school program. Some of the measures relating to aptitude and other characteristics of children are designed to serve classroom teachers in guiding activities for specific pupils, including individualization of instruction, by determining reasonable expectations of achievement and in identifying pupils who need diagnostic study or remedial instruction. Finally, guidance officers use these test results in order to foster realistic self-perception in pupils and to help boys and girls select educational-vocational goals as well as choose appropriate courses of study.

However, it is important to recognize that counseling itself is nonevaluative, nonjudgmental. Although tests are instruments of evaluation, they do not make the counselor a judge, for he uses examination results to assist his client, the student, in evaluating him-

---

* From Pitirim Sorokin, "Testomania," *Harvard Educational Review*, Vol. 25 (1955), p. 199. Reprinted by permission.

self. The ultimate purpose of tests and indeed the purpose of counseling, is not so much to help the guidance person understand the client—though this is necessary—as to help the student understand himself. Confusion about this ultimate goal of counseling has led to a misunderstanding about the place of data and information in guidance services. It is not what the counselor knows about the client but what the client knows about himself that is most important, because the student must make his own decisions and therefore his own self-evaluation (2).

It would be erroneous to assume that most of a counselor's information comes from test scores; indeed, personal interview is the major technique used to identify pupil difficulties. Guidance persons must therefore be good listeners. Most of us find it hard to listen to one another because each of us is thinking about what he wants to say. This kind of listening, listening to have one's say in turn, is not the kind that is conducive to good counseling. Rather, listening should not be a passive thing but an active following of what the client is saying, and the student should be given complete freedom to talk, to tell his own story without interruption. In other words, through the interview, the guidance counselor is not trying to get at the facts alone though they be important, but to see the problem as the client sees it, to understand his perception, his feelings.

Some persons have questioned the advisability of using interview techniques with youngsters from the slum, especially children who are retarded in some phase of their educational program. While it may be true that it is more trying to work with those who lack verbal facility, a counselor, if tactful, can derive valuable information from most children if he affords them time to speak their mind. When children who are emotionally upset exhibit sarcasm or defensiveness, the counselor does not consider himself the victim of a personal affront, nor does he retaliate to show who is boss. He accepts the child as he is, knowing full well that rudeness is a weak man's imitation of strength.

Through personal conferences with pupils, the counselor can assist classroom teachers in curriculum planning and assignments. Especially where educational retardation obtains, his awareness of aptitudes and abilities can result in drawing implications for program modification and change. His working with the teacher can improve the suitability of assignments and classroom experiences for those most in need of success. Then too, adjustment problems in the class-room can be reduced by a close relationship between counselor and teacher. This is especially true in the case of new pupils who arrive to find a strange environment, are met with new demands, and are unfamiliar to their peers. Introducing newcomers to the school and acquainting them with procedures and requirements calls for an experienced and understanding person if tensions are to be lessened and anxiety diminished.

The counselor's responsibility for vocational guidance has recently received increased priority. As ever-rising work requirements are established even for initial employment, it becomes essential that youngsters adequately prepare themselves for an appropriate place in the labor market. The need for helping adolescents to make a wise choice of occupation cannot be overestimated, as one's career decision may determine his future prospect of success and happiness, social class and place of residence, style of life and working hours, outlook and values. Work thus involves the whole person, influencing his total personality. Ann Roe writes, "If one wishes to understand the total psychology of any person, it is at least as important to understand his occupational behavior as it is to understand his sexual behavior" (3).

Children of the slum often have difficulty deciding what kind of work to prepare themselves for. In general, low-income parents lack cognizance of their child's ability and possess only a limited familiarity with work types. The most common familial response is either to dismiss the issue or to urge adoption of aspirations that are unrealistically high. Although teachers may be aware of the youngster's potential, they too lack knowledge about possible labor alternatives. In fact, Lifton (4) found that the knowledge of teachers about occupations was inversely related to the distribution of jobs, knowledge of the professions being greatest. That children are just as unlikely to receive direction from textbooks is shown by a survey indicating that there is an emphasis on the service occupations in the primary grades and a rapid shift to the professions in the upper grades. Thus, many children receive a distorted picture of the labor market, so that when asked what they want to do in life, they appear to be unrealistically biased in choosing professional jobs (5).

Perhaps the best career decisions are predicated on the help a trained counselor gives pupils in assessing the elements vital to an intelligent selection. Frank Parsons, father of vocational counseling, made the process clear when, in addressing a youthful audience, he indicated three broad factors that enter the choice of a vocation: (a) a clear understanding of oneself, and one's attributes, abilities, ambitions, resources, limitations and their causes; (b) knowledge of the requirements, conditions of success, advantages and compensations, opportunities and prospects in different lines of work; and (c) true reasoning of the relations of these two groups of factors (6).

Although the province of guidance has recently been extended to include elementary children, some educators maintain their belief that counselors are not needed in the early grades because no vocational choices are made at that level. However, this belief is inconsistent with knowledge concerning development of personality, for the causes of most difficulties arise in childhood. Were more guidance available at that time, it might well serve as preventive mental health treatment. As the responsibility for counseling services expands, so too the competence and degree of involvement of its personnel must increase. A 1961 study of the state of Illinois revealed that 47 percent of the counselors in that state had no more than one semester of training in guidance; 45 percent of the counselors were devoting less than half of their time to guidance and counseling (7). Certainly in the future we need a greater number of well-educated specialists in this field. At the 1960 White House Conference on Children and Youth, two of the resolutions were, "That the number of pupils per counselor in secondary schools be decreased from the present ratio of 625:1 to 250:1," and "That the ratio of students to elementary school counselors be 600:1." During the interim before these ratios are achieved, the teacher's task is not to lament the shortage of services but rather to make wise use of those services that exist (8).

SOCIAL WORKER

Teachers newly assigned are likely to be dismayed by the frequency of pupil absence, tardiness and truancy. Not only does poor attendance result in a diminution of class progress because the teacher is obliged to repeat the same lesson on several consecutive days, but an academic deficit accumulates for those pupils who consistently miss important learning experiences. Increasing attention is being given to the factors which promote recurrent absence, the causes for staying out of school, the reasons for skipping. Educators have come to recognize that nonattendance is a symptom indicating some problem in the child, his home, or the school, and that a youngster who chooses this way of expressing a difficulty should have as skilled help as does a child who exhibits symptoms of disturbance in other ways.

When student problems involve peer exclusion, academic frustration, or other matters indigenous to the classroom, the teacher may be able to remove barriers obstructing progress. But when the difficulty stems from aspects of child life extrinsic to the school, teachers cannot be so helpful. Some boys and girls may be out of class because of household chores or babysitting while parents work. Or, unknown to his family, the child may be downtown with other out-of-school children. In short, as the reasons precipating nonattendance are many and varied, resolution may well be contingent upon an investigation of home life and out-of-school activity.

Ever since they were first included as members of the educational staff, social caseworkers (sometimes called visiting teachers or home counselors) have performed an invaluable service to the school, its patrons, and parents. Under the leadership of social workers, educators have been led to see the inappropriateness of limiting professional services and attention to pupils who are in attendance while confronting those who stay away from classes with an attitude of crime and punishment. An increasing number of states are finding the visiting teacher helpful in resolving problems of nonattendance as she relates to teachers her insights concerning home conditions, attitudes of parents, parent-child relationships, habits of eating and sleeping, the way children spend their leisure, and causes of tardiness and absence. At times the social worker is able to make helpful suggestions regarding adjustments in curriculum, materials of instruction, method, and social relationships in the classroom (9).

Usually children come to the attention of a social worker by referral from teachers, principals, parents or social agencies. As she is familiar with numerous dimensions of difficulty that are involved in nonattendance, the caseworker attempts to determine what factors are precipitating the symptom. Her initial task is to ascertain whether pressures extrinsic to the child are fostering his absence or failure.

To what extent and in what ways are these results due to factors within the individual? When and how did these problems begin? Is their origin recent or are they long established? What is their etiology? Subsequent to a situational diagnosis, the visiting teacher attempts to register change in those elements of home or school life that appear to be obstructing pupil achievement. Usually her efforts on behalf of the boys and girls are welcomed, but in some instances of parental neglect the home counselor finds it necessary to protect youngsters by interpreting social expectations and legal demands to adult surrogates. As liaison between parent and teachers, she is able to convey school purpose and progress to the home and, conversely, to relate the familial point of view to educators. When children inaccurately report classroom expectations and processes to their parents, the visiting teacher is usually able to rectify misunderstanding and thereby sustain the positive relationship between home and school.

Working with slum families can be a taxing responsibility. Because many parents lack carfare or clothing to go out of the neighborhood, work under inflexible schedules, or have an illness at home or little children to care for, it becomes necessary for caseworkers to arrange appointments at the pupil's residence. Even then there is the possibility that one may not find parents at home or that parents may arrive late because few own a watch or attach any importance to punctuality. Ordinarily the only time the entire household is present is in the evening or on weekends. While this is an inconvenience to the school social worker (especially with prevailing rates of over 1,000 pupils per social worker), it is also the best alternative, because it promises a situation in which she may see the parents, observe interaction among family members, and take note of role expectation and performance.

Where help required by families with several problems is unavailable in the school services, social workers must be familiar with other community agencies in order to suggest an appropriate type of assistance. Depending on the specific need, help may involve budgetary or homemaking service, financial support, referral for medical care, psychological testing, family relations counseling, or psychiatric assistance. Even when a choice of agency has been made, the caseworker must take the initiative in setting up the appointment for the child because parents may lack interest or the know-how necessary to perform such a task. Other responsibilities incumbent upon the visiting teacher include consultation with professionals from nonschool organizations who share a common concern for the same child. Together they work toward the promotion of child guidance—to reveal to troubled children and troubled adults who are conscientious in the discharge of their responsibilities toward youngsters under their care—new possibilities of adjustment which lie within their reach. Juvenile delinquency, behavior disorder, preventive mental health treatment—these also are important factors of the caseworker's comprehensive role (10).

Up to now the functions of guidance workers and visiting teachers have been both coincident and complementary. Whereas counselors have performed most of their duties at the secondary level, the social caseworker has emphasized service in the elementary school. One essential difference distinguishes the context of these two groups of specialists; namely, most social workers feel that the focus of their effort should be directed more toward parents than children; guidance counselors indicate that a greater part of their time is spent with children than with parents. Both of these emphases are needed to keep the teacher informed. To know the child, the teacher must know the home; and to know the home, she must either visit a pupil's residence or rely on the observation and experience of the social caseworker. The prospect of visitation is unlikely when one considers the increasing inschool demands being made of teachers; the wisdom of relying on caseworkers becomes apparent when one is familiar with their skills and proficiency.

SCHOOL NURSE

Few of us perform with optimum efficiency when our physical condition warrants attention. Because there is a relationship between health and achievement, most school systems now employ registered nurses as professional staff members sharing the common interest of helping children receive a better education. The emphasis of the basic role of school nursing has shifted recently from first aid and the exclusion of pupils with contagious diseases to the interpretation for parents and teachers of health information about specific children. Primary functions of the nurse now involve appraising student health to detect remediable physical problems, counseling parents and teachers regarding examination results, and assisting the home in obtaining adequate treatment or correction. In slum neighborhoods, where the young are least apt to receive proper care, the school nurse is a very important person.

At the outset of every school year the nurse screens each pupil for remediable difficulties. By far the most common health problem among low-income children is dental caries. Many of these boys and girls have never been to a dentist before entering school, and as most of us know, it is difficult to be attentive when preoccupied with pain. Children of the poor also make up a large proportion of the 7.5 million youngsters in this country needing eye care and the 1.5 million who have a hearing impairment (11). Nurses report that slum pupils frequently complain of stomach-aches that occur because of insufficient diet, undernourishment, malnutrition. The crowded low-income home with continuous television viewing from morning until late at night tends to deny adequate amounts of sleep and exercise to its entire membership. Some pupils have diseases of the scalp such as head lice, or diseases of the skin such as impetigo; many are ill-clothed, lacking coats, hats and overshoes and seem to catch every cold that comes along.

Providing teachers with a checklist of things to watch for in the classroom can facilitate identification of health problems that might not be revealed by cursory screening. For example, does the child squint? Can he see the board? Does he hold the book close to his face while reading? Does he turn his head to hear you? Is his skin clear or unusually blemished? Does he appear restless, sleepy, or lethargic? In their periodic conferences, nurses and teachers discuss this information, transfer it to a cumulative or health card and initiate whatever action seems appropriate. The important thing here is that just as the teacher depends on the nurse to assist in diminishing factors which obstruct learning, so too the nurse must depend on the teacher for referral and the observation to identify students in need.

In most neighborhoods the school nurse has no difficulty soliciting parental support and cooperation when there is doubt about some aspect of the child's health. A phone call to the home explaining that Johnny is squinting and showed up poorly on the Snellen Vision Examination, with a suggestion that a careful check by the family physician is in order, usually brings quick assistance for the child and completes the nurse's task. However, in slum schools, nurses face the perplexing assignment of contacting parents and convincing them that their youngster is in need of health care. Ordinarily it takes at least three times as long to get a slum child to a doctor as it does a child living elsewhere. For one thing, there may be no phone, or the mother may be busy working, physically ill, or having another baby. Written correspondence seldom is effectual as many of these families are reluctant to open an official-looking envelope lest it contain a bill. In fact, many slumdwellers pick up their mail only when expecting a check. To send a note home with a child requesting the mother to come in and visit brings the reply, "Sorry, busy." If the nurse delays too long, the child may be gone, for families often "get lost" by moving in and out of the neighborhood when rents are due. Having exhausted all other means of communication, the nurse usually must go to the child's home. There, amidst the loud crying of small children and the blaring television, she must impress upon parents their responsibilities as well as the pupil's need (12).

Convincing the parent is one thing, but getting the child to a clinic is another matter. An appointment must be arranged which does not conflict with family plans; it cannot fall on the day clothing is given out by the church or Salvation Army, the day another child in the family has an appointment elsewhere, or the day mother works. Even after the nurse has arranged a referral so as to coincide with parental schedule, some mothers arrive late or do not meet their appointments. The usual excuse is, "No one could have gotten the other kids up for school if we had to be at the clinic by 8 A.M." or, "Why get there at 8 A.M. when they never call you into the office until 11 A.M. anyway?" or, "I didn't have the 50 cents carfare for the clinic, we'll go next time." Thus, even though a community organization may supply funds for free eyeglasses, a youngster whose next time may not come until it's too late shows up in school the following day squinting, unable to see the board, ill-equipped to get the education that should be his.

After repeated attempts to motivate parents, the school nurse often requires the assistance of the visiting teacher. On an issue vital to a child's health, such as frequent absence because of an infectious condition, the nurse and social worker visit the student's home so that the legal violation "contributing to a minor's delinquency" may be understood and care rendered without delay. Another cause for joint effort occurs when children arrive at school having been physically punished so severely that their well-being is jeopardized. In these cases, the nurse, school social worker and legal authorities must intervene. Similarly, this conjunctive effort must occur where cases of sex offense arise. In one midwestern high school last year, 30 pregnancies were reported. While this problem is not exclusive to slums, it does occur in greater frequency there than elsewhere and in numerous cases is unrelated to consent. A member of the extended family, a friend of the home, or a neighbor may force sexual relations with a young girl. Together the visiting teacher and nurse help parents see the need for providing the expectant mother with prenatal care and bring legal forces to bear upon those responsible for her condition.

In many schools the nurse is a member of the guidance team, confidante to children who solicit her advice about personal problems of mental health, morals, hygiene and sex, that they might not wish to speak about with a counselor. It has been suggested her training background and relation to children should qualify the nurse to enter more into school instruction. Unfortunately, few nurses are sufficiently equipped to teach health classes. In 1962, only 10 percent of the 550,000 professional nurses employed in this country had an academic degree and only one fifth of that group of 10 percent held a graduate degree (13). Consequently, responsibilities for health education are usually consigned to the physical education instructor, who may have a health science major, or another teacher who has specialization in biological sciences. But the nurse does contribute to the instructional program by assisting teachers in activating pupils to acquire healthful habits, informing the faculty about health and disease through inservice meetings, and counseling teachers about needed adjustments in the physical environment of the classrooms.

With an average ratio of 2,000 pupils per school nurse, there is likelihood that each day the nurse will confront youngsters who are in need. This often means more contacts to make, forms to fill out, another mother to motivate. Most of the nurses do this without complaining, and they do it well, because, like the teachers who remain in the slum, they love the young poor.

BUILDING PRINCIPAL

The extent to which teachers are successful in classrooms and satisfied with their working conditions depends in part on the role assumed by their building principal. Ordinarily administrative appointments to the central city are made only to persons who have demonstrated understanding and empathy for the disadvantaged; persons who are cognizant of learning and behavioral difficulties; persons who have shown enthusiasm and success in working with inner-city staff and low-income parents. As most of these school leaders perceive their major function to be that of coordinating staff efforts, they are keenly aware that their attitudes about education, their expectations of teachers and students, and their relationships with colleagues can greatly influence pupil progress and success.

An effective principal consistently identifies himself with the major problems confronting teachers, even though this consumes much time. He is aware of the demanding nature of their roles and seeks to facilitate instructional tasks in any way possible. His interest and concern for mutual effort with instructors is perhaps the key which permits an able administrator to serve as liaison between the faculty and the professionals who offer special services. Perhaps it also distinguishes him from fellow administrators who are less effective because they see the principal role as one of "running the store." It is not uncommon, as complexities of the school increase, for some administrators to become oblivious to the real aims of their institution. The mechanics of operating a large plant with many personnel sometimes can overwhelm the principal so that he comes to perceive his function only in relation to decisions regarding managerial efficiency and gives little or no attention to the educational process, to the learner, or to those who teach. Needless to say, organization should never precede purpose if effectiveness is the goal.

Administrators also gain the respect and confidence of the staff by maintaining realistic classroom expectations. Under the auspices of the National Commission on Teacher Education and Professional Standards, a conference on the problems of urban educators was held in October 1964 at Washington, D.C. At these meetings some twenty inner-city teachers, representing eight metropolitan centers, were given an opportunity to express their views as to how building principals could assist them to provide more effective instruction, better working conditions, improved morale. Several of the recurring complaints issued by the participants follow:

1. "The administrator lacks compassion."
2. "Principals forget what it is like to be in a classroom."

3. "Principals make unrealistic demands for achievement in order to enhance the institution's reputation." (14)

Participants agreed that there should be no administrative expectation that all or even most children will measure up to grade level, since in a normal population group, this is to expect an arithmetic impossibility. Similarly, all children ought not to be expected to finish a prescribed textbook. When such demands are made, the teacher is forced to choose between meeting obvious pupil needs and requiring goals that cannot be met. The effective principal relies on his teachers' judgment to maintain realistic outcomes for individual pupils; he mediates his expectations by encouragement rather than threat, support rather than dictate.

If principal and teacher are to work effectively with one another, their rapport should be based on mutual effort rather than the relationship in which the administrator's function is primarily teacher evaluation. The new instructor, the teacher working on tenure, the educator who is unsure of his ability—these persons will not solicit help if to do so is to subject oneself to a rating or an evaluation. It is when principals forget this proper relationship with their staff that the chance to help is diminished. Bertrand Russell said it well: "The teacher, like the artist, the philosopher and the man of letters, can perform his work adequately only if he feels himself to be an individual directed by an inner creative impulse not dominated and fettered by an outside authority" (15).

The principal's function as liaison between teachers and supportive staff is perhaps his most important responsibility, one which he will be able to fulfill only if he provides a context of emotional support, maintains realistic expectations, and relates in a friendly way to the staff. However, beyond the principal's prospect as a coordinator of services, certain measures that can ameliorate working conditions also are within his province. He cannot diminish class size or provide materials which are unavailable, but he can successfully confront one of the biggest problems that face teachers: namely, nonteaching duties, excessive work loads which require that one devote a substantial portion of class time and out-of-school hours to routine and nonprofessional activities. One research effort (16) shows that over one hour of the teacher's time each day is spent in carrying on activities such as correcting papers, marking reports, putting materials on the board, taking role, performing housekeeping tasks, and collecting funds—activities that do not call for a high degree of professional competence. A 1962 study of the National Education Association reveals a similar picture of the time teachers devote to noninstructional activities (17).

Undoubtedly the workload of the teacher has a direct relationship to his efficiency; when extra hours of energy are consumed, effectiveness is necessarily reduced. Teachers claim they need more clerical help and monitorial assistance—people to copy some of their reports for them and to assume some of the nonteaching duties. By utilizing the dedication of his Parent-Teacher Association, by contacting local universities for the use of teacher aides, by working with community and civic groups, the principal can provide clerical assistance to staff members and, in so doing, lessen their load to allow time for consultation, time to teach.

SCHOOL SUPERINTENDENT

Whereas a building principal may be proximate, accessible and well-known to his teachers, this situation seldom obtains in the case of the school superintendent, who might be located in another part of town and seen by the instructional staff on rare occasion only. Yet, as removed from classroom problems as he might appear, the superintendent has perhaps the greatest potential influence for improving instruction and working conditions of any single person in the system. As an advisor and executive agent of the board of education, chief administrator of the system, and leader of the staff, the superintendent occupies the focal point of responsibility within a system.

Whether a superintendent does assist teachers by reducing class size and nonteaching duties, providing needed materials and facilities, or improving salaries and morale can depend on the extent to which he is aware of the needs. Obviously each teacher cannot be queried in person as to his complaints, difficulties and suggestions. Rather, through staff advisory committees related to issues regarding instruction, materials, evaluation and personal welfare, the administration is kept up to date. When faculties choose vigorous, informed leaders to represent them in meetings with the central office, they usually benefit. It is unfair to lament a superintendent's lack of judgment in matters on which the teachers have provided him an ill-informed representative, a person chosen solely because of his willingness to attend a meeting. The matter of selecting appropriate delegates cannot be overestimated.

From his confrontations with staff groups, the superintendent determines appropriate action. His special contribution lies not in possessing more knowledge than others in the system but in judging which demands are most crucial, which needs of greatest moment. Essentially his is a decision-making position in that, as advisor to the board of education, he must continually assess the priorities of staff requests and grievances. But a superintendent's support of his teachers is not confined to interaction with the board of education. He can foster public understanding of the school system's strengths and weaknesses, of particular problems his teachers face, of their achievements, and of the truth that their task requires nothing less than overcoming obstacles that the entire society has failed to overcome.

That the foregoing responsibilities for supporting school staff are incumbent upon all chief administrators is shown in a 1963 policy statement by the American Association of School Administrators of the National Education Association, entitled *This We Believe.*

> We believe that the superintendent has a responsibility to see that opportunities are provided for staff members, teachers, supervisors, principals, and specialists, to play appropriate roles in developing personnel policies and maintaining professional working conditions.
>
> We believe that the superintendent has a responsibility to assist staff members in ways satisfactory to them in studying welfare problems, in developing proposals pertaining to staff welfare, and in presenting them to the school board for consideration and action.
>
> We believe that failure to find appropriate and acceptable means of involving staff members, teachers, principals and supervisors, in developing policy that directly affects them will lead to divisiveness, tension, and conflict that will impair the schools and adversely affect the education of children. (18)

Among administrators who are cognizant of the problems of inner-city teaching, the most common response is a commitment to improving working conditions. This can begin in a small way by something as simple as providing safe parking in an unruly neighborhood. In planning a new budget, consideration may be given to obtaining part or full-time services of more social workers, psychologists, psychiatrists, nurses, dentists and guidance personnel. In schools where individual differences exceed the limitations of regular classroom instruction, additional staff may be hired to work with small groups of retarded or emotionally disturbed pupils. Assistance in handling disruptive children may be extended to allow teachers more time for individual attention to other class members. The superintendent can revise the roles of supervisors, consultants and helping teachers when necessary, so that less emphasis may be placed on evaluation and more attention given to consultation, aid and assistance.

Overcrowding is perhaps the greatest problem of the moment to teachers insofar as working conditions are concerned. They report that excessive class size reduces the amount of individual attention given to pupils and all but eliminates the practice of using democratic methods in the classroom. In the quest for better pupil-teacher ratio, it is important for instructors to recognize that class size may be contingent upon factors extrinsic to administrative choice. For example, the shortage of teachers in some cities affects workload and class size. In Philadelphia there are presently 1,100 teacher vacancies; in New York City, 1,300. Certain systems report difficulty in recruiting qualified instructors; Baltimore indicates that 21 percent of its 1963–64 staff have not met certification requirements, as compared to only 8 percent of the staff in 1954–55 (19). Similarly, nearly 7,000 of the 45,000 teachers in New York City are substitutes (20). Then, too, that overcrowding tends to relate to some subject areas more than others is illustrated in Philadelphia, where the mathematics and science areas need 52 percent more teachers than are now employed. Inadequate facilities also may necessitate larger class assignments. In New York City, class size has been reduced, but in a way which lessens learning time: while double sessions diminish the number of pupils in a class, they also decrease the number of hours that youngsters spend in school. East Orange, New Jersey, and other cities are employing the educational plaza concept in an attempt to equalize opportunity and to offer instructional groups of reasonable size. The plaza concept of locating nearly all educational facilities in the center of the city seems feasible for communities of small area with high population density. Finally, finance can be an overriding influence. In Washington, D.C., from 1950 to 1960, while the total city population was decreasing 5 percent, the school population grew 20 percent. The oppressive paradox that resulted in the nation's capital was the superintendent's necessity to provide better education for an ever-growing number of pupils out of a proportionately declining budget.

Regardless of the cost of eliminating overcrowding in classrooms, our major cities soon must lessen the number of pupils assigned to teachers if we hope to educate youth properly in the slum. The Educational Policies Commission of the National Education Association has recommended a class size of 20 pupils or fewer per teacher in disadvantaged neighborhoods: 50 professional staff for each 1,000 children (21). At this writing, no major city has been able to comply with the Commission's suggestion; to do so is the urgent responsibility of each superintendent. Until the commitment to providing inner-city youth a real opportunity for learning is made good, the attainment of an adequate education is unlikely for some, dubious for others, impossible for many.

BOARD OF EDUCATION

Although members of the board of education are not part of the school staff, their decisions have a significant effect on educational programs, working conditions, and teacher morale and success. About 85 percent of the laymen who serve as board members (known in some states as *trustees, committeemen,* or *directors*) occupy their office by election. The remaining 15 percent are appointed by a civil authority such as the mayor, city council, or county commissioners. Contrary to modal selection, board members in half of the cities with populations over 500,000 are appointed to their roles (22). As the prerogative to create or abolish boards of education resides with each state legislature, there is considerable variance among the sovereign units, so that what is mandatory in one state may be only permissive in another, and expressly forbidden in a third. Even within a state the legislature can grant different powers to varying types of districts.

In general, however, the board has far-reaching powers involving personnel selection and employment, choice of texts and course of study, establishment of teacher salary and inservice education, building construction, and determination of class size.

For school board members to render the best possible judgments, they must bear in mind community expectations, school needs and staff welfare. When these interests do not coincide, the board is subjected to conflicting group pressures and subsequent to decision making receives censure and criticism from those whose purposes are not served. On the one hand, there are a multitude of lay organizations representing business, industrial, service, and patriotic groups, whose interest is indirect but nevertheless real when concentrated on public education and the schools. On the other hand, there are organizations of professional educators, whose direct and primary concern is with improving curriculum, instruction, and learning. Only by affording each collective voice a hearing can the board members attempt to encounter and resolve these pressures in the best interest of children. To their credit it should be indicated that most boards do an admirable job.

Usually the most substantial contact board members have with the views and judgment of teachers occurs when there is organized representation of the staff. To be sure, the superintendent's role includes an accurate reporting of teacher needs and requisites, but the local teachers association also has a responsibility for mobilizing board support and assistance. Without representation, teachers in the central-city schools cannot make known their need for diminished class size, reduction of nonteaching assignments, improved facilities, additional assistance from specialists—time to teach. Whether pupils' and teachers' needs will be served depends in large measure on how their case is presented to the board, the philosophy and purpose of the teachers' association, the kind of relationship prevailing between board members and association leaders. At the present time two major groups vie for the opportunity to represent classroom instructors in matters of professional growth and welfare: the American Federation of Teachers and the National Education Association.

Regardless of which organization teachers choose to be affiliated with, it is important to strive for a paragon in staff-board relationships. Certainly a first step toward this elusive goal involves the selection of teacher representation that is firm but not militant, intelligent but not officious, professional in every sense of the word. The local association's obligation to inform the board accurately about slum school conditions requires that information related to pupil needs for professional services, smaller class size, remedial instruction, and materials be carefully documented. Especially is this necessary in the case of new board members, who, unaware of difficulties peculiar to the low-income area, might be prone to deny budgetary exceptions. An effective representative can also be helpful in reminding board members that the education of children is dependent on the character, ability, and dedication of teachers more than any other factor, and that to be effective, teachers must be provided a work schedule and load which allows time for individual pupil attention, time and opportunity for growth in service, and time for consultation with specialists.

Teacher proposals are more likely to receive favorable board consideration when prefaced by a history of cooperative activity and good faith. To assemble with the board only as issues of teacher welfare arise is an evasion of professional responsibility. By working in concert throughout the year on other matters that affect child well-being, both the board and the teachers association come to understand better each other's functions and difficulties. In this context teachers not only solicit board support when school critics are in season but reciprocally defend board judgment when it is construed in an unfair manner.

The association can inform its members about current fiscal problems which the board must encounter. Education presently receives only 2 to 3 percent of America's wealth. Not long ago, 80 percent of the tax dollar was collected and spent in local districts, but today a reversal has occurred, so that the federal government now collects and spends nearly 80 percent of the American tax dollar, leaving only 20 percent to local districts, counties and states. Despite this revolution in tax collection, more than 90 percent of the cost for elementary and secondary education is still borne by local districts, counties and states on the national average (23). This imbalance between the collection agency and the agency paying for public schools would seem to indicate a need for basic change in our thinking about support for education (24). During the interim, while boards must deal with the issue as best they can, teacher understanding and support seem appropriate.

EPILOGUE

Some will question the rationale for excluding a description of the school psychologist, reading instructor, speech therapist, librarian, placement counselor, or others of the staff. They have been omitted not because they perform tasks of lesser importance than any other specialist considered here, but rather because the limited purpose of this chapter has been to indicate how the functions of supportive staff members in general can assist both the teacher and the pupil in facilitating personal and academic achievement. Even the roles indicated here for each professional are not comprehensive, nor were they intended to be. In sum, the attempt has been to diminish walls of misunderstanding and apprehension that can deter a teacher from sharing his responsibility of helping youth reach their potential.

The character of our society—its strengths, integrity, effectiveness, freedom—is definitely determined by the degree and quality of its individual members. That character is never static: it is either improving or deteriorating. Only as the staff of slum schools work together, utilizing every talent and strength among their members, can the prospect of low-income children be encouraging.

RESOURCES

(1)   Sorokin, Pitirim, "Testomania," *Harvard Educational Review,* Vol. XXIV (1955), pp. 199–213.

(2)   Patterson, C. H., *Counseling and Guidance in Schools* (New York: Harper & Row, Publishers, 1962), pp. 149–64.

(3)   Roe, Ann, *The Psychology of Occupations* (New York: John Wiley & Sons, 1956), p. 31.

(4)   Lifton, W. M., "Vocational Guidance in the Elementary School," *Vocational Guidance Quarterly,* Vol. 8 (1960), pp. 79–81.

(5)   Patterson, *op. cit.,* p. 191.

(6) Parsons, Frank, *Choosing a Vocation* (Boston: Houghton Mifflin Company, 1909), p. 5.

(7) State of Illinois, Office of the Superintendent of Public Instruction, Board of Vocational Education, Occupational Information and Guidance Service, *Development of Guidance Services, 1959–1960* (Springfield, 1961), mimeographed.

(8) Golden Anniversary White House Conference on Children and Youth, Recommendations 196, 197 from proceedings, Washington, D.C., March 27–April 2, 1960.

(9) Strang, Ruth, *Pupil Personnel and Guidance* (New York: The Macmillan Company, 1940), pp. 295–97.

(10) Kurtz, Russell H., ed., *Social Work Yearbook, 1957,* Thirteenth Yearbook, National Association of Social Workers (New York: American Book-Stratford Press, 1957), pp. 509–12.

(11) Patterson, *op. cit.,* p. 256.

(12) Busenberg, Eliza R., Personal communiqué from Mrs. Busenberg, Chief Supervisor of Health, Board of Education, Columbus, Ohio, October 10, 1964.

(13) American Nurses Association, *Facts About Nursing* (New York: The Association, 1963), p. 7.

(14) Strom, Robert D., "Ideas to Take Home," in *The Urban Association's Responsibility for Recruitment, Preparation, and Inservice Education of Big-City Teachers* (Washington, D.C.: National Commission on Teacher Education and Professional Standards, National Education Association, October 1964), pp. 14–16.

(15) Russell, Bertrand, "The Functions of a Teacher," *Harper's,* Vol. 181 (June 1940), p. 16.

(16) Central Michigan College, Special Studies Department, *A Cooperative Study for the Better Utilization of Teacher Competencies* (Mt. Pleasant, 1953), p. 28.

(17) National Education Association, Research Division, "Time Devoted to School Duties," *National Education Association Research Bulletin,* No. 40 (October 1962), pp. 86–87.

(18) American Association of School Administrators, *Roles, Responsibilities, Relationships of the School Board, Superintendent and*

Staff (Washington, D.C.: The Association, a Department of the National Education Association, 1963), pp. 12–13.

(19)   Berwick, H. Orville, "Notes on the Baltimore Public Schools," paper prepared for the National Commission on Teacher Education and Professional Standards meeting on *the Urban Association's Responsibility for Recruitment, Preparation and Inservice Education of Big-City Teachers,* Washington, D.C., October 2, 3, 1964, 3 pp., mimeographed.

(20)   New York City Board of Education, "Facts and Figures on New York Public Schools," abstract presented to the National Commission on Teacher Education and Professional Standards meeting on *the Urban Association's Responsibility for Recruitment, Preparation and Inservice Education of Big-City Teachers,* Washington, D.C., October 2, 3, 1964, 2 pp., mimeographed.

(21)   National Education Association, Educational Policies Commission, *Education and the Disadvantaged American* (Washington, D.C.: The Commission, 1962), p. 23.

(22)   Tuttle, Edward M., *School Board Leadership in America* (Chicago: Interstate Printers & Publishers, 1963), pp. 147–56.

(23)   *Ibid.,* p. 84.

(24)   Morse, Wayne, "Federal Support for Education—Now and in the Future," in *A Financial Program for Today's Schools* (Washington, D.C.: Committee on Educational Finance, National Education Association, 1964), pp. 17–24.

> *The secret of education lies in respecting the pupil.*
>
> —*Emerson*

Classroom Instruction

5

Most of us agree that for a teacher to deny a child understanding and affection is to deny him an education. Without these elements of response, the slum child will reject school as he rejects life outside the institution. Nonetheless, some of us persist in maintaining higher priority for concerns of how teaching proceeds than of how learning occurs. As a consequence, the perfection of individualized instruction has been perceived as simply a matter of lower pupil-teacher ratio, better systems of grouping, and more time per child. Certainly something more than increased time and organization is needed to effectively instruct those who appear disinterested, their fellows who are belligerent, others who are slow and the remaining host of differing personalities in each classroom. What is required is a greater knowledge of learners and the learning process, more appropriate diagnostic measures to determine scholastic weakness, and methods of teaching that are in conjunction with each pupil's most efficient learning style and pace of accommodation. In short, what is called for is the highest form of respect: understanding.

TYPOLOGY OF LEARNING

For many years there was only one method of teaching because it was assumed all learning occurred in the same manner. Indeed, both mode and content of education during the late nineteenth and early twentieth centuries were dominated by theorists who fathered a scientific miscarriage known as *faculty psychology*. The rationale began with the premise that mind is the mental correlate of body and that therefore, just as the body has physical qualities, so the mind must possess psychical qualities. Each of the 35 mind attributes such as memory, judgment, and understanding were known as faculties. As to strengthen the body requires muscular exercise, the mind's faculties were believed to be strengthened by exercise through practice and drill. Teachers were assigned the arduous task of exercising those faculties in which strength was desired. Some curricular subjects, because of their difficulty, were deemed better exercisers than others. As a consequence, mathematics and Latin became the sine qua non of learning.

The aim of education was to produce a highly trained mind, not necessarily a good one. Knowledge and practical information were thought to come through experience after the mind had been properly trained, disciplined, and strengthened. The more difficult the school tasks, the better suited to this end they were thought to be. Such a view tended to keep practical, useful, and interesting subject matter out of classrooms because it apparently would not produce the show of painful effort by students which more abstract and abstruse mental puzzles could evoke. Effort and difficulty became in a way the standard for judging the educational value of a subject.

Because each faculty apparently was unique in rate of growth, it was assumed that each could best be trained at a different age. Memory, for example, appeared teachable at an earlier age than reason, so young children might be expected to memorize but not understand. Early memory training would furnish raw material and provide an adjunct to reason when the latter faculty came to be exercised in later years. Thus, in history classes emphasis was on remembering famous names and dates rather than on understanding cause and significance of events. Similarly, geography stressed the ability to locate obscure and unimportant places rather than the gaining of insight as to the effect of land and sea upon man's life style.

Under faculty psychology, learning was simply a physical exercise of supposed compartments in the mind. Students did not understand, they absorbed. In the learning process, the student was viewed as reactive, not active; he did not think, he listened. Indeed, listening was equated with learning. Even furniture was designed with this in mind: immobile desks held one's body, if not one's attention, in place. Fortunately, the faculty concept died as experimental psychologists showed that there could be a faculty for each situation in life (1).

Modern research indicates that not all learning is a matter of physical exercise or memory, that practice and drill are not the only modes which facilitate growth, that intellectual development and the "disciplined mind" are not necessarily synonymous. Rather, it now appears that there are at least several dimensions of learning—skill, knowledge, attitudes—each of which may differ from others in structure and in the methods most effective for its accommodation. For example, whereas physical skills like football and golf requiring a high habit content for proficiency might well be developed through practice and drill, these methods are ineffectual when applied to teaching knowledge, the intellectual dimension of learning.*

By viewing the several verbal pictures which follow, one can readily appreciate the importance of teaching knowledge by problem-solving techniques rather than by rote, memory, practice, drill. First, we look in upon a group of early elementary pupils whose instructor has assigned them a series of manipulative tasks. Before the period began, this teacher helped his students select problems that would be appropriate to their individual levels of development. As they work about the room, some in groups and others by themselves, these children are learning by doing; that is, through activities of manipulative construction they come to recognize cause-effect relationships, foresee consequences of action, organize conceptual schemes by determining what leads to what, and experience the joy of discovering knowledge. In short, they are gaining understanding. Only as each pupil comprehends the solution to his problem does the teacher's role become one of communication. She then relates the name of the

---

* From *The Tragic Migration* by Robert D. Strom, pp. 30–31. Copyright 1964, National Education Association. Reprinted by permission.

activity, the process, or the parts of the task to the child. By providing him a vocabulary, the teacher gives meaning to a pupil's understanding, gives him words that he can use to express what it is he knows. This sequence of providing understanding as a preface to vocabulary is vital for intellectual development. Otherwise the undesirable result is a pupil who can say more than he thinks or knows, has more words than ideas—a verbalist.

The danger of reversing understanding and vocabulary in the learning process is well illustrated in a story often told by William James of Harvard. The eminent psychologist was visiting a classroom in which children were being taught by the catechetical method. After a period of observation, James requested an opportunity to pose an inquiry. He asked, "If I were to dig a hole down into the center of the earth, would it be colder or warmer there?" None of the students responded. Interrupting the silence, their teacher suggested that they knew the answer but the question was improperly framed. Upon her query, "In what state is the interior of the earth?" a bevy of hands went up, and the respondent chosen said, "The interior of the earth is in a state of igneous fusion." What did the pupil possess— understanding or words, knowledge or verbal report?

When children are helped to develop understanding and then acquire vocabularly to describe what they know, a third aspect of learning necessarily ensues. The pupil is able to synthesize his learning, organize his experience, and continue to grow even after he is out of the classroom and teachers are no longer available. Unfortunately, the teaching method of some demonstrates a belief that the three steps of cognitive learning (understanding, vocabulary, synthesis) can be reversed so that instruction may proceed from synthesis to vocabulary to understanding. For example, consider the classroom in which it is assumed that children do not need to understand number relations or combination outcomes. Here arithmetic lessons begin with knowledge that is already organized, synthetized and embalmed in a textbook. Under this procedure, the first step in a typical encounter with a new mathematical process, say multiplying fractions, is to memorize the universal rule for multiplying fractions. Next, practice and exercise in applying this rule to derive answers are assigned to ensure that every pupil knows the operant routine. Very often adherence to this method results in a child's confronting his mentor with, "I know how to do it but do I use multiplication or division?" Does such a child really know how to solve the problem? Does he understand number relationships and mathematical structure, or does he simply know the mechanics of following an arithmetic rule? The reader who is reluctant to accept what all of us suspect applies to our own early training can try this problem. If asked what the rule is for dividing fractions, most of us could remember to invert the divisor and multiply. Let the reader ask himself, why?

In those whose elementary arithmetic is taught by rote, drill, practice, by memorizing someone else's learning rather than by understanding numerical relations and combination outcomes, there usually develops an antipathy to mathematics when, in later grades, progress is solely contingent upon comprehension. Often the little boy who could do well in memorizing his multiplication tables, although he knew nothing of the integral associations involved, finds that he cannot be an engineer, a doctor, or a physicist because higher mathematics, which requires the unalterable requisite of understanding, is closed to him. The Illinois Math, School Mathematics Study Group, Minnemath and other recent curricular programs represent a healthy transition.

It seems that there is a point in the hierarchy of knowledge above which one cannot ascend if all his learning is memory based. A

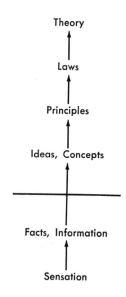

rudimentary construct of knowledge, from its lowest form, sensation, to its highest, theory, is shown here. As one ascends this ladder of knowledge, he cannot proceed beyond the realm of facts and information on a rote background. Above that level, conceptual structure is vital, seeing relations is paramount, understanding is indispensable. Certainly we admire those of our number who live above the context of facts and information; in the future, social and occupational survival will demand that more of us do so.

Given the importance of problem solving, one might expect this learning dimension to occupy a primary position in both classroom and homework instruction. However, mental discipline remains the major objective for out-of-school assignments; many pupils who cannot be successful during class are directed to return the following day with a specified number of problems completed. Usually this is done neither in malice nor because teachers are more interested in having things done than in having them learned, but because a belief persists that practice will promote intellectual learning and that the discipline of finishing tasks will develop personal responsibility as well as culminate the learning process. The truth is that for pupils who fail to understand lessons in school, homework assignments only serve to alienate or further frustrate. In some cases an actual displacement of fulfillment occurs in homework: the teacher rather than the learner is pleased with the completion of assignments. A feeling that her authority has been accepted and her responsibility dispatched, the teacher may receive an ill-founded sense of accomplishment and self-satisfaction. To say the least, it is lamentable when student work proceeds not for personal growth and fulfillment but to please or propitiate an instructor.

Perhaps the greatest problem concerning homework today is that more often than not answers are what is evaluated rather than the process used to derive solutions. Rather than an emphasis on determining why a pupil is getting wrong answers, we assess how many errors are made. Obviously, students soon learn that the most important thing is to write *finis* to one's paper. As the product is what is evaluated, the student, in his eagerness to finish, employs shortcuts rather than appropriate processes. This action encourages not only careless haste but an attitude of completing one thing and getting on with another, until finishing becomes a veritable compulsion and the pupil comes to view that which he has completed as his achievement.

If, in fact, problem solving is the objective of intellectual tasks, it ought to be given more than perfunctory attention in evaluating achievement and progress; otherwise homework is not instructive, it cannot be diagnostic, it is without positive significance.

Just as the methods of practice and drill, appropriate for learning skills, prove questionable when applied to teaching knowledge, so they are abortive in attitudinal tutelage. Attitude learning differs from both skills and knowledge in that it is attached to emotion and learned primarily through emotional experiences rather than by problem solving or practice. Upon reflection, it is manifest that behavior is often determined more by how we feel than by what we know. Nevertheless there are those who attempt to teach attitudes in the same manner as skills—by habit or compliance. Adult insistence upon certain behavior which is ethically correct will usually bring incorpora- tion of the desired reaction—but only for the moment and super- ficially. Some believe that if a child is forced to be correct even though not sincere, he will soon be both. Unfortunately, biological and ethical maturity are not parallel. Many people grow up but never become adults. It is true that a child will adopt behavior directed by his elders temporarily, but his purpose is to gain approval or avoid punishment. For consistent moral behavior, a method more effective than parental dictate or teachers' orders must be used to create and reinforce a positive attitude of youngsters toward the desirable behavior.

Identification is superior to compliance as a goal in the attempt to inculcate attitude sets. As the sense of self strives to emerge, young- sters attempt to pattern their personality, their life response, after an adult model whom they wish to resemble. Each of us tends to emulate and imitate those whose admired behavior appears satisfy- ing and desirable to us. Since answers to personal questions are sought in the behavior of one's model, this character must be in- volved in similar circumstances in order to provide contemporary direction. This presents a difficulty in the slum because the most succesful models we might choose for these children have moved away. The usual recourse is to stress biographical reading about those who, now famous, were slumdwellers in their youth.

Adolescent interaction represents a potential vehicle for incul- cating desirable attitudes in slum children. Cultural anthropologists are now predicting that the amount and nature of the ways children learn from one another will increase. It is likely that the rate of instructional change will be so great that children being born at this time will find few patterns of behavior in the present adult population that will stand them in good stead when they reach maturity. Hence, children may be forced to turn more and more to each other in working out effective and satisfying patterns of action. Therefore, an attempt is being made to determine ways by which adult-desired attitudes can be introduced to youngsters through the peer group with its powerful influences and sanction, but not in such a way as to activate reticence about adult intrusion—teaching kids through kids, a model within.

LEARNING STYLES

Not only is instruction influenced by difference in types of learning but recent studies suggest that children differ in their preference of learning styles. It seems that inquiring, exploring, and testing are every youngster's "playpen curriculum" and mode of development until the time of entrance to school. Then the rules are switched, and the pupil becomes a dependent learner waiting for teacher cues. Evidence shows that some children adopt the authoritative method of learning in which one accepts something as true because some person of repute says so. This authority may be a teacher, parent, textbook, encyclopedia, or newspaper. On the other hand, some children remain committed to the spontaneous style of learning in which trial and error, experimentation, and idea modification are utilized. Empirical data seem to indicate that many things, though not all, can be learned more effectively and economically in creative ways than by authority. Indeed, many individuals whose preference for creative learning is especially strong tend to make less educational progress when we insist that they learn by authority. The field of creativity, more than any other, opens exciting possibilities for making individualized instruction a reality.

The current emphasis on creativity stems from an expanded concept of mental functioning. It is no longer widely believed that memory, vocabulary, number facility, and general reasoning are the composite of man's abilities. Instead there is now rather general acceptance regarding the importance of the creative thinking abilities which include fluency (the ability to produce a large number of ideas), flexibility (the ability to produce a variety of ideas or use a variety of approaches), originality (the ability to produce ideas that are unusual), elaboration (the ability to fill in details), and redefinition (the ability to define or perceive in a way different from the usual, established, or intended way). That these aspects of intelligence are not measured on current I.Q. tests is shown by the fact that if we identify as gifted only those people scoring in the upper 20 percent or an I.Q. exam, we would eliminate 70 percent of those who score in the upper 20 percent on a measure of creativity.

Although the creative thinking abilities have only recently come to the attention of educators via psychology, these abilities have always been important in thought production. In her study of 300 acknowledged geniuses, Catherine Cox of Stanford University (2) has estimated their probable intelligence quotients on the basis of early mental traits. According to Dr. Cox, the estimated I.Q. of persons like Molière, Heine, Balzac, and Sir Isaac Newton was 120 to 130—ratings that are surpassed by a large proportion of freshmen in a number of colleges today. Were high I.Q. alone equivalent to creative talent, we would graduate thousands of Sir Isaac Newton's each year.

If the quest for creativity is to be successful, classrooms must operate in conjunction with Edward Thorndike's law of effect: that "behavior which is satisfying tends to be repeated." Only as creative behavior is accepted, encouraged, rewarded, and satisfying can it be expected to flourish. Conversely, when pupils find that imaginative endeavor is unacceptable, out of bounds and subject to disdain, their only recourse is to pursue whatever action context appears most likely to bring reward. To ensure minimal resistance to the development of inventive functioning, it is important to examine some of the needless ways by which teachers inadvertently drive the creative process off course.

In questioning teachers from several countries regarding the characteristics of ideal pupils, E. Paul Torrance (3) found that almost all educators want the student to be obedient and industrious. They find most objectionable talkativeness, disruption of class procedures, and guessing. These least desirable learning attributes personify the creative person, whose independence may make him appear rebellious, whose conceptual style may seem to suggest he is playing around, whose capacity for complete absorption in work may lead others to view him as antisocial. Guessing is to him a first step in the scientific method of inquiry, because the creative thinker is committed to intuitive and inferential speculation. He may be talkative, especially during a question period, when, because of his persistence to find an answer, his behavior is perceived as disruptive. For example, consider the teacher who attempts to read Mother Goose rhymes to a small group of young children. As soon as she tries something like "Tom, Tom, the Piper's Son," the inquisitive youngster starts interrupting: "Was Tom about my age? What is a piper? Was Tom's father poor? Is that why Tom stole the pig? If Tom was my age, how did he carry a pig? If the pig was so small, how did it kill a goose? What's a calaboose? You mean they put little boys in jail?" At this point, the teacher is liable to say, "Forget it. Either you be quiet and stop interrupting or I will quit reading." When a consistent derogation confronts curiosity and questions, it is unlikely that such components of behavior will persist.

How divergence is handled in the classroom can affect development of the creative process. If a pupil runs the risk of censure, criticism, or ridicule from teacher or fellow students whenever he asks an unusual question or advances a new idea, it is likely that his deviance will soon be replaced by conformity to behavioral norms of the group. Indeed, in some cases the creative person whose learning style differs from that of his peers may actually feel guilty about his talent if others do not accept it, if the use of his abilities precludes social acceptability. An example of this guilt reaction is shown in a story written by an imaginative pupil who participated in the Minnesota Tests of Creativity. When called upon to conjure some fantasy about a monkey who could fly, this youngster produced the following:

> Once there was a little monkey who was always doing what his mother told him not to do. One day he told his sister, "I can do something that you will never be able to do. I can fly." His sister said he couldn't, so he climbed the tree, gave a leap and began to fly. His sister ran as fast as she could to the mother monkey. The mother was surprised and angry. She told the little monkey to go back to the house but he refused. So that night when father monkey came home, the mother told him all about it. And he went out and got the little monkey and said for him not to fly any more or all the other animals would think he was crazy and out of his head.

A point of interest and concern is the fact that while social expectation for behavioral conformity obtains in most cultures, the amount, source, and kind of pressure differ from country to country. Not all societies are equally supportive of creative behavior; they vary in the amount of individual divergence allowed. For this reason, the Minnesota studies (4) included an investigation of the attitudes of different cultures toward divergency. Thousands of children from Canada, Greece, and the United States were requested to write imaginative stories about animals or persons with some divergent characteristics. It was believed that these materials would reveal each pupil's perception of the ways his society deals with those who differ from the group. In the American narratives, the source of pressure tended to be the pupil's peers, whereas in Canada and Greece, it was society in general. The forms of pressure in the American stories were ridicule, laughter, coercion, and isolation. In the stories of Negroes attending nonsegregated schools, pressure came in the form of hostility, violence, ridicule, and coercion. On the other hand, the Greek stories evidenced pressure primarily in the form of questioning (Why are you different? Do you understand our way? Why do you prefer to deviate?). Similarly, the Canadian emphasis was on understanding the causation of differences. Little such concern was manifest among the American stories which took the attitude that divergency is divergency and cause matters not. As most of the American pressures come through peers, it seems feasible that teachers could be of assistance to creative youngsters by demonstrating tolerance and acceptance of differences in the classroom.

Another clue as to how creativity is thrown off track comes from the kind of tests being given in the classroom. An examination of evaluation methods used at all levels of education during the early twentieth century indicated that an overwhelming number of tests were memory based, demanding only recall of information. Looking at current tests, one finds that the emphasis has shifted to recognition, which essentially calls for acquaintance and familiarity with materials. Rarely do tests call for thinking of any kind—divergent, critical, evaluative, or convergent. Because grades are important to children, they will tend to learn whatever is necessary to obtain the desired mark. Therefore, if evaluation is based on detailed memorization, students will memorize. It follows that if the emphasis is on ability to apply and relate principles, pupils will attempt to develop this ability. That change is the lot of tomorrow's adult is certain; the result of change is equally uncertain. Precisely because this is true, our schools must abandon the concept of retention as the epitome of educational purpose.

By imposing stereotyped sex roles on children, we constrict their province of experience, their creativity. When boys come to believe that only the "sissy" is open to feelings, interested in form, color, movement and ideas, certain aspects of potential are denied. Similarly, when girls feel that it is inappropriate for them to be intellectually curious, interested in exploration and experimentation, creative growth is hindered. An openness to experience is one of the most striking characteristics of highly creative persons. This was recently demonstrated at the California Institute of Personality (5) where, on a number of tests of masculinity-femininity (so called by Carl Jung, who postulated the male experiential emphases to be thinking and sensation as opposed to the female role of feeling and intuition), some 600 creative males scored relatively high on femininity. Nevertheless, as a group they do not present any effeminate appearance or give evidence of increased homosexual interests. Rather, their elevated scores on femininity indicate considerable receptivity to the experiential realm of feelings and emotions—important elements in the creative behavior of either sex.

Another threat to creativity occurs when fantasy and imagination are discouraged and originality and inventiveness are declared off limits. Under these conditions, the mind has nowhere to go but to the obvious, the safe, the commonplace circuit of authority learning. The fact that most children arrive in elementary school with tremendous creative potential makes it imperative to provide many opportunities for solving problems, for imaginative role playing, and for keeping fantasy alive until intellectual development is adequate for a sounder kind of creative thinking. Pretending should be legitimate until abstraction can absorb the imagination's force and demonstrate the power of originality in adult-accepted form.

The creative abilities of slum children have often been overlooked because their curiosity does not express itself in well-phrased query; they initially manifest little desire to work independently; and they seem to experience difficulty in putting ideas down on paper. In the latter instance, we have sometimes interpreted halting action as an index of retardation, although in fact many inventive persons whose ideas come more quickly than the pen's facility find writing difficult. To activate latent creative abilities of low-income pupils, we must be reluctant to interpret initial limitations as being necessarily predictive of learning possibilities. In many cases, unique learning patterns will emerge only as a reversal occurs in adult response to certain elements of behavior. That is to say, where imagination and ingenuity have previously been abandoned because of punishment at home or in school, these components will cease to be dormant only as they are revered, encouraged, and rewarded in the classroom.

Teachers can encourage creative thinking by respecting unusual questions and ideas, and by helping children develop powerful skills of inquiry—especially how to sustain, refine and test a hypothesis. By recognizing value in creative ideas, adults can also support the inventive process of youth. For example, there may be occasions when, upon offering an unusual idea or suggestion to the class, creative children are subjected to an immediate jeer by their fellows. Precisely here the teacher can intervene by calling attention to the potential of this unacceptable idea and asking the class to help further refine it. As pupils assist in developing a concept and its implications, they come to respect its author, recognize the need to consider carefully ideas that have not been precisely framed, and realize that their teacher does respect originality. That many of us do not believe children can produce ideas of value is shown by an evaluation emphasis on recall, recognition and reproduction to the exclusion of creative thinking, decision making and problem solving. Because which types of learning children pursue usually depends on the kinds of examinations given, it is important to ensure a compatibility of purpose between teaching and testing.

Creative process is stimulated also when thinking is made a legitimate classroom activity; when periods of nonevaluative learning are permitted; when recognition is given to the fact that not all learning is expressed in verbal form; and when the teacher relationship to the pupil is primarily one of support. One of the biggest problems in life for the creative youngster will be getting along with others without sacrificing the qualities that make him original, inventive, and different. The teacher may be able to assist him in using his sensitivity to be kind and his insight to be understanding and tolerant of those who do not see things his way. She may be able to help him realize that he can assert himself without being domineering, work alone without being withdrawn, and be honest with others without being overcritical. By respecting the creative youngster, the teacher can enable him to accept the fact that anyone who has original ideas must be prepared to be a minority of one, at least for a time.

THE SLOW LEARNER

An important component within the matrix of style is learning pace. For teachers throughout America, there is perhaps no problem of greater concern than that of the so-called *slow learner*. This unsatisfactory term has come into general use to designate anyone equipped with less than average capacity to learn. Usually students are so classified when, on repeated measures of scholastic aptitude, an I.Q. between 80 and 95 is indicated. The relation of this problem to school instruction comes into sharp focus upon recognition that one child in every five is a slow learner (6). This means that public schools have the task of providing education for more than 8 million less able pupils, whose presence is felt in almost every community in the United States (7). As might be expected, the proportion of slow learners is markedly higher in slum schools than elsewhere.

Slow learners are not to be confused with educationally retarded youngsters of average or above average intelligence who might be emotionally disturbed. Nor should they be considered stupid because slowness of pace often indicates only that one is extremely meticulous, cautious and careful; that he refuses to generalize easily; or that he cannot understand concepts without doing something physically, such as grimacing, shifting posture, moving hands, or making other paralanguage movements. For the most part, however, the slow learner goes through substantially the same mental processes as his average or rapid classmate. It is important to recognize that the slow learner may require that directions be repeated, since his memory component is not always strong. Also, these pupils need time to finish tasks, more time than other students. The slow learner needs goals which are proximate, activities in which sustained effort is not required for success, initial learning opportunities in which enthusiasm need not always be accompanied by tenacity.

Though any youngster, given adverse circumstances, might be a potential dropout, children categorized as slow learners could most be considered *predictive dropouts,* since it is from their I.Q. range more than from any other that pupils leave school before graduation. Reasons for leaving school given most frequently by such students are lack of interest, inappropriate curriculum, and inability to maintain acceptable grades. Under these conditions, it appears that to affirm the inability of a slow learner while lamenting the pupil's disinterest and failure is the least effectual stance educators can assume. A more positive view would involve working toward increased educational effort for less able pupils by providing them a realistic curriculum, especially in those content areas that they indicate are least relevant and most difficult for them—reading, social studies, and mathematics.

Reading. In homes of the culturally handicapped, language is not a tool. It may be a threat; it may possibly be nonexistent as a medium of communication. Often one finds that the maximum exposure to language has come from the television set—a source by which a pupil is exposed to torrents of language, used in context unfamiliar to him. In addition, no response is expected of him; he is merely an observer, not a participant in the communication process. Among other attitudes such a student lacks is the realization that the viewer should do some of the work. He does not realize either the nature or the extent of participation a receiver must bring to the process.

Usually the slow learner is introduced to formal reading before he is ready. Because his life is lacking in conversation and his home is devoid of magazines, it is difficult for him to read words he has never heard or understood. At the University of California Institute of Human Development, Holmes and Singer approached the reading readiness problem from the standpoint of a substrata factor theory (8). By their research, 75 percent of the specific abilities contributing to reading power were identified. The following subvariables account for 64 percent of the factors resulting in competent reading performance.

1. Knowledge of vocabulary in context, 16 percent.
2. Ability to understand verbal analogies, 16 percent.
3. Auding, defined as the ability to manipulate verbal symbols which are heard, 16 percent.
4. Knowledge of vocabulary in isolation, 16 percent.

All of these factors require in common the ability both to recognize and use language as a symbolic system—perhaps the most basic difficulty that the culturally handicapped child has. It is little wonder that the academic experience of such a student begins in frustration and ends in failure because success depends on his mastery of the tool of reading and mastery of reading depends on verbal experience.

Breaking down the primary variables, researchers found that one factor, range of information, accounted for major portions of the four basic subabilities. This second level factor contributed

1. 38 percent to ability to understand verbal analogies,
2. 38 percent to auding ability,
3. 43 percent to knowledge of vocabulary in context,
4. 52 percent to knowledge of vocabulary in isolation.

Certainly all would agree that the range of information of culturally handicapped children is limited, in some cases to the immediate neighborhood. Therefore, what is most needed is a readiness program that provides students many experiences with words, including visual and auditory discrimination; with the concept of language; and with the idea of communication before they tackle the task of reading. Encouraging in this regard is the increasing number of kindergartens and preschool centers.

The necessity for reading readiness as an integral part of the curriculum is implicit in the assertion that more than half of all inner-city children are one or more years behind their counterparts of the suburb in reading. Were the validity of this assertion ever in doubt, it is again confirmed by performance of slow learners on the California Capacity Questionnaire administered in San Francisco's Reading Laboratory. Here students ordinarily score from 10 to 40 points higher or nonverbal sections of the examination. Then, too, pupils recommended for the special reading laboratory seem to have no difficulty with mathematics courses so long as study does not require word-problem analysis. There is, for about three-fourths of the slow learners, a marked difference between achievement by grades in verbal subjects and that in nonverbal courses such as mathematics, art, music, and some shop or sciences (9).

In short, the greatest problem in the area of reading and language arts for the predictive dropout is not whether to use the Fernald method of teaching kinesthetic learners, the Spaulding Unified System of Phonics, or the specific language disability method of Gillingham; it is the establishment of readiness as an integral part of the curriculum.

Social Studies. According to dropouts, social studies is among those courses considered most difficult. Yet it is precisely in this curriculum area that the pupil is to develop understandings and attitudes vital to his success in society. Here he is expected to make such important gains as an understanding of himself and of his place in the community and an enthusiasm for the learning process. Unfortunately, the content area is too broad to be covered adequately by all students, so that urgency of time and schedule tempts teachers to provide an excess of ready-made explanations for the less able pupil. This results in lost opportunities for him to develop abilities in independently gaining insights into concepts. The result of teaching small parts of a large number of topics is the passive reception of disconnected ideas, not illuminated with any spark of vitality. It might be better for the slow learner if ideas were fewer in number but presented in a variety of combinations to facilitate the use of intelligent inferences and analogy.

Social studies curriculum, more than any other, can be based on the social characteristics and needs of the pupil himself. The slow learner often accepts uncritically the leadership with the greatest emotional appeal and he may be either belligerent or obsequious in dealing with persons in status positions; therefore social studies should emphasize important qualities of good leadership, intelligent selection of leaders, and the choice of courses of action based on probable effects rather than on emotional appeal. To curb a tendency to be prejudiced toward people who are different or who hold other points of view, the social studies should stress common characteristics of mankind, helping the pupil to understand why racial, cultural and political differences exist. Feelings of inadequacy and exposure to peer rejection may be diminished in classrooms where the value and understanding of human dignity is developed by respecting the ability of all groups to contribute to society.

Since not until adolescence do most children develop the sense of time which is required for historical perspective, it is safe to assume that this sense comes even later for the slow learner. In some measure, social class background can influence this issue, for the middle-class child appears more able to see the past and is working with the present to achieve goals of the future. In this he is in contrast to the lower-class child, who tends to be interested only in the present and what is immediate in his environment. Yet the social studies should give some concept of the vast sweep of history and prehistory as well as the sense of space and variation which characterizes the planet and its peoples. The direct effect of time and space on the pupil as an individual often needs to be established. An example of this on the secondary level is the development of units which first identify the pupil with an issue and establish its significance to him, then place the issue in its historical and geographical setting, and conclude with a return to the here and now where the issue is associated with current affairs of national and international significance (10).

The slow learner will be a voting, reacting, working citizen. He will need to know about his own drives and physical needs and his relationship to his home, community and nation as an elementary school child, as an adolescent, and as an adult. He needs to know basically how the government which affects him operates and what part he plays in its effectiveness. He needs to know how and why people in other times and places affect him. He needs to know in what ways his environment is different from that of others. Above all, he needs to know why his role in society is essential to others.

In the last years of secondary school, social studies can be closely related to occupational preparation, providing opportunities to put into practice many of the social attitudes and understandings gained in prior years. This phase of the social studies must be taught by a skillful, perceptive teacher who can recognize realistic opportunities to develop concepts but who can also enable the pupil to identify principles and practices that will increase the effectiveness and satisfaction of his existence.

Mathematics. Particularly in mathematics, where learnings are cumulative, the slow learner may soon fall hopelessly behind if pressured to keep pace with average or above average members of his class. Studies have shown that the slow learner goes through substantially the same mental arithmetic processes as his favored peers, except that he seems to have a different rate of perception and moves at a slower pace. Consequently, he often needs a lengthy period in which to grasp or understand what is to be learned. Also, success or failure in mathematics is closely related to a pupil's ability to develop the reading skills required for the subject. In a sense, mathematics is a language of its own, calling for careful perusal with a high degree of comprehension. Therefore, study during primary years should include an extended readiness period for the introduction of quantitative concepts along with a basic vocabulary for numbers. The normal sequence of arithmetic skills can be pursued if it is adjusted to the individual's rate of learning with no grade standards as criteria.

Success of modern mathematics programs with less able pupils suggests that the discovery method is appropriate. Studies in New York City indicate that students low in scholastic aptitude profit relatively more from the School Math Study Group program than do pupils in upper brackets. This may be largely due to the fact that the program brings into play kinds of abilities not especially useful in mastering traditional materials. Edward Begle, head of the Stanford Math Study Group, reports that his organization, which has done more than any other to modernize mathematics, will shortly begin considering how to teach youngsters who have fallen behind in racially segregated and slum schools.

The junior high school predictive dropout is, for the most part, neither ready for nor interested in learning about such topics as taxation, banking and interest; such learning should be reserved for the senior high school years when there is greater likelihood of immediately using it. This does not preclude the use of practical mathematics in junior high school. However, the content should reflect adolescent experiences such as aspects of part-time employment, wages and hours, travel distances, measurements of athletic fields, lapses of time, and recipe ingredients.

In senior high school also, mathematics should be directly related to industrial arts and home economics experiences. As the pupil is guided toward occupational fields, his mathematics instruction should be directed toward proficiency in specific areas, including consumership and taxation. At the same time, programs should maintain basic understandings which allow for adjustment to varying situations requiring computational application. In its entire range, the program should provide not only the understanding of fundamental processes in mathematics but the recognition of their social application for the effective solution of quantitative problems in daily life.

There is reason to be optimistic concerning occupational training in the secondary school for all pupils who require it, whether they be slow or fast. Even before passage of the Vocational Education Act of 1963 (Public Law 88–210), a number of school systems had begun to offer such new preparatory courses as custodial services;

shoe repairing; cosmetology; laundering; valet service; nurse's aide work; duplicating services; painting; decorating and furniture refinishing; lawn and garden care; small appliance repairing; auto mechanics; file clerking; family services; and food preparation. Furthermore, the U.S. Department of Labor is providing leadership in regional programs to ensure that curricular change is in accord with manpower needs. However, though a vocational course of his choice might readily sustain the interest of a predictive dropout, there remains the task of engendering his interest in those curricular areas to which all pupils are exposed before occupational training. It is precisely here, in reading, social studies and mathematics, that antipathy or enthusiasm is nurtured, success or defeat is sealed, dropout or retention is determined (11).*

LEARNING AND EVALUATION

Those who would respect others must necessarily refrain from making prejudgments. It follows that to assess individual achievement in a classroom before the learner has an opportunity to demonstrate advance is to discredit the instructional process, deny academic progress, and disrespect the pupil. In response to charges that intelligence tests are middle-class oriented and so penalize slum children, that I.Q. scores influence teacher attitude and unduly fix student classification, the New York City school system and others have recently discontinued the practice of administering group measures of scholastic aptitude.

Those whose agitation secured the "test ban" contend that youngsters fortunate enough to score a high intelligence quotient in the early elementary grades will tend to be favored throughout their school career because teacher expectation for each pupil is usually derived from this singular source. Hence, those who score low are less likely to be recipients of teacher encouragement, favor, or individual help, since their prospect for the future does not appear good. Moreover, since the I.Q. is often viewed as a predictor of success or failure, teacher reactions to individual test scores can transfer to

---

* From Robert D. Strom, "Toward Realistic Curriculum for Predictive Dropouts," *The Clearing House*, Vol. 39, No. 2 (October 1964), pp. 101–106. Reprinted by permission.

grading in the classroom. As a consequence, when a child who scores low appears to achieve much, the product may be considered luck. On the other hand, a high scoring child usually receives good grades even when achieving at a low level, either because the teacher assumes extrinsic factors have caused his inadequate performance or simply because it would be difficult to justify a low grade to a youngster of high I.Q. because of possible parental repercussions.

If the limitations of intelligence tests were more widely known, it is likely that fewer pupils would be prejudged by their I.Q. scores. Since it has been a time-honored practice to establish validity in new measures of intelligence or scholastic aptitude by determining how closely performance on them correlates with performance on the old Simon-Binet or its revisions such as the Stanford-Binet, it has been difficult to break away from too narrow a conceptualization of the human mind. We have been trapped by the definition that "intelligence is what intelligence tests measure." The dilemma here is that validity refers to evidence of correlation with an existing measure of the same function. There is no doubt that all intelligence tests of high validity measure the composite of mental functions. As recently as 1959, J. P. Guilford conceptualized mental functioning to include cognition, memory, convergent production, and evaluation, each of these operating on four content types and six kinds of products. Yet, although some of these functions are not measured in old tests, new examinations measuring them cannot depart too far lest they lose validity.

There is little doubt that we have depended far too much on intelligence tests to measure mental retardation and giftedness. They have always been the sole instruments used in assessing intellectual potential and mental growth. Unfortunately, we have usually shaped our educational curriculums and methods to bring about only the kinds of growth and achievement that are related to the mental abilities involved in intelligence or scholastic aptitude tests. The tragedy of this procedure is clear when we recognize that an ability gradient operates concerning I.Q. measures. That is to say, if one has enough of whatever abilities are measured (say an I.Q. of 120), having more than enough (over 120) is not as important as having some other abilities, such as those considered in tests of creative thinking—fluency, flexibility, originality, elaboration and redefinition. The narrow concept of the human mind and its functioning has produced a kind of learning experience which falls far short of our ideal of a humane education that will give all children a chance to realize their potentialities.

But prejudgment is not the only obstacle to meaningful academic evaluation. Equally deleterious are those situations in which the context for success is so structured that achievement is rendered impossible for certain pupils. While most of us favor "healthy competition" in life, there is much unhealthy school evaluation that goes under the guise of this acceptable term. Competition can only occur within a range of uncertainty—that is, the range in which both success and failure are possible. It cannot occur where each participant does not have a chance, where the outcome of victory or defeat is predetermined. The result of a comparison between the work-product of a pupil whose I.Q. is 85 and of another's whose I.Q. exceeds 130 ought to be a foregone conclusion. In a sense, school "competition" becomes a daily punishment for those of lesser ability. Under circumstances in which few participants have a chance to win, it is not strange that numerous students protect themselves by setting a low level of aspiration—that is, by not trying (12).

Meaningful assessment of achievement is also denied in classrooms where all pupils are urged and expected to reach identical goals. That standards in schools would rise if every student were required to demonstrate competence in his grade level before advancing to the next class is a common proposal of those who lack an understanding of the term *grade level*. Many children are victimized by instructors who fail to realize that grade level is a statistical concept describing the midpoint in the achievement levels of a typical group of students. The term guarantees by definition that half of any normal group of pupils will achieve at grade level or above while the other half will achieve at grade level or below. To expect all or even most children to reach grade level or above is to expect an arithmetic impossibility. One might as well argue that 90 percent of those who marry should be women (13).

Even where educational purpose and expectation are in conjunction with student potential, the term *individual achievement* remains a misnomer unless instruments designed to measure achievement can assess personal growth. Many classrooms follow tradition which dictates that pupils should be measured by comparison with others, even though our knowledge of learners and the learning process has revealed that the valid measure is one which assesses growth of an individual in relation to his previous position. Under present methods of operation, achievement in the classroom is communal rather than personal.

Assessing achievement by group standard may be likened to the efforts of an Arkansas farmer who sought to determine a fair price on the pig he was placing for sale. In order to determine the weight of the pig, he balanced a long pole across the back fence. He tied the pig to one end of this pole and attached a large gunnysack to the other. He filled the gunnysack with rocks until pig and rocks were of equal weight, and the pole was again in balance. Then, to determine the weight of his pig, the farmer estimated the weight of the rocks.

To nullify individuality as a criterion for marking is to negate the validity of grades themselves if their purpose is, in fact, to record individual progress. To employ group curves as the standard for an individual's achievement is to guess the weight of the pig or, in our instance, the achievement of the individual. In both cases, we assign a pseudo-weight after first weighing something other than that with which we are concerned. It is fair to say that the concept of individual differences has been employed least in the area where it is most needed: in the assessment of achievement.

Leaders in some school systems are now considering the prospect of developing more relevant, accurate and meaningful measures of evaluating achievement. Marking systems tell the majority of children that they are mediocre, some that they are failures, and others that they are doing all there is to do—all of which is likely to be erroneous. This prompts questions about both the motivational effects of marks and the basis of their determination. Should grades be used at all if they tend to distract students from desired educational objectives, if poor grades tend to discourage further attempts at learning, if good grades tend to cause future laziness on the part of the student? Should grades be based on effort, improvement, performance, or some ultimate standard such as grade level? At this juncture, the only thing clear is that there is no clarity in these matters.

The indication of one promising direction for a new rationale comes from the New Haven, Connecticut, schools, where there seems to be a movement toward locating the goal of the educative process inside the process itself: growth is its own end. Since growth is personal, progress can no longer be determined apart from the individual. In this context, pupil self-appraisal in conjunction with teacher guidance becomes a more legitimate and tenable base for the evaluation of achievement than any judgment from external sources. Until now educators have been more interested in what is taught students than in what students learn—the rationale followed that only a teacher can properly assess what advance students make. This idea is no longer tenable, for the verb *educate* is not just transitive, it is also reflective; it is not something we do to the child but rather something the child does to himself, a noetic process. Perhaps part of being educated is to determine or to evaluate one's own advance, to know what one knows and what one needs to learn to satisfy oneself for mental well-being and vocational success. If knowledge is really subjective and therefore unique, it might be best evaluated by its possessor. With the aid of diagnostic tests and increased teacher guidance, self-evaluation becomes a healthy possibility.

In conclusion, most slum children will grow in proportion to the respect we as teachers have for them. Whether their stature will become that of responsible adults and useful citizens depends in large measure upon classroom training. At its best, teacher respect will be demonstrated by adapting instructional methods to fit pupil style, pace, and learning type. By establishing an academic environment in which pupils can achieve, maintaining expectations that are realistic and using methods of evaluation that relate to personal growth, we can be more successful in low-income neighborhoods. Some wish to be told that to reach these goals is either easy or impossible; in truth, the task is both difficult and possible.

RESOURCES

(1)   Strom, Robert D., *The Tragic Migration* (Washington, D.C.: the Department of Home Economics, National Education Association, 1964), pp. 29–30.

(2)   Lagemann, John K., "How We Discourage Creative Children," *Redbook* (March 1963), p. 124.

(3) Torrance, E. Paul, "Are the Gifted Being Challenged to Think Creatively?" Paper presented to Sacramento State College, Association for Gifted Children, Sacramento, California, October 14, 1961, p. 13, mimeographed.

(4) Torrance, *ibid.,* p. 16.

(5) MacKinnon, Donald W., "What Makes a Person Creative?" *Saturday Review* (February 10, 1962), p. 16.

(6) National Education Association, Research Division, "Education of the Slow Learner," *Research Memo,* No. 18 (Washington, D.C., June 1964), p. 2.

(7) Kephart, Newell C., *The Slow Learner in the Classroom* (Columbus, Ohio: Charles E. Merrill Books, Inc., 1964), pp. 158–278.

(8) Holmes, Jack A., "Speech, Comprehension and Power in Reading" (Berkeley: University of California, 1964), mimeographed.

(9) Abbott, Mary K., "The Culturally Handicapped and the Reading Process" (San Francisco: Public Schools Community Improvement Project, 1964), pp. 1–3, mimeographed.

(10) Newell, Lillian, "Developing Concepts in Social Studies" (San Francisco: Public Schools Community Improvement Project, 1964), pp. 1–4, mimeographed.

(11) Strom, Robert D., "Toward Realistic Curriculum for Predictive Dropouts," *The Clearing House,* Vol. 39, No. 2 (October 1964), pp. 101–106.

(12) Strom, Robert D., "Academic Achievement and Mental Health," *Journal of Secondary Education,* Vol. 39, No. 8 (December 1964), pp. 348–55.

(13) Frymier, Jack M., "Ninety Percent Should Be Women," *Education,* Vol. 84 (April 1964), pp. 498–500.

> *All that is necessary for tyranny to triumph is that good men do nothing.*
> —*Edmund Burke*

Prospects

6

Most discussions about the future of slum communities engender an element of skepticism. Educators (1) who fear that the environmental trap of poverty will continue to expand indicate that the proportion of culturally deprived children in large cities has increased from 1 in 10 (1950) to 1 in 3 (1960) and is projected to reach 1 in 2 by 1970. Other schoolmen believe that a problem of more ominous dimensions is the rising incidence of juvenile delinquency. Already adolescent disorder has spread to school classrooms, where periodic eruption of hostile display lends credence to the image of the inner-city school as a blackboard jungle. As this picture deters many teacher candidates from electing or accepting a position within the core city, so-called "difficult" schools must operate with an increasing number of less trained, more inexperienced instructors. Another problem about which one cannot help registering alarm involves reports of ascending dropout rates, which even now exceed 50 percent in certain neighborhoods. Equally discouraging are the findings of Project Talent, revealing that in some pockets of poverty over 90 percent of the 18-year-old students rank among the lowest 10 percent of their age mates and far below the average level of unskilled industrial workers in general educational achievement (2). From whatever vantage one assumes, the future of the slum appears to be a repetition of its past.

Children of the poor are more likely than their middle-income peers to reach adulthood unskilled, ill-educated, and unemployed. Though slumdwellers may have the desire and willingness to work, these are insufficient job qualifications for the future. Among young people under 21 years of age in urban depressed areas, there has been a 50 percent unemployment increase over the past five years, a 20 percent increase in the past year. Our current rapidity of change, which dictates obsolescence, is shown in the fact that man has doubled his knowledge in the past decade; over half of the known discoveries in science and technology were made by persons who are still alive. In response to the knowledge explosion, new occupations are emerging which require more extensive preparation by those who wish to work. Perhaps the most significant factor influencing the unemployment crisis has been that machines, which at the turn of the century did 6 percent of our work, now do 96 percent. To be sure, machines are cheaper than people; they reduce human relations problems by reducing personnel; they improve business procedures with almost instant feedback of information; they increase efficiency because distance is no longer a barrier to control and coordination. But they also replace about 4,000 workers in this country every week (3).

The tragedy of desire without competence is shown in New York City, where 54,000 jobs are available but go unfilled for lack of qualified personnel, while 77,000 out-of-school unemployed youth look for work. A similar example is Cook County, Illinois, where nearly 270,000 persons are on public assistance. Fifty percent of the Chicago reliefers cannot read at the eighth-grade level; over half of them are under 32 years of age and because of their youth may be expected to produce another generation of dropouts. According to Raymond M. Hilliard, director of public aid for Cook County, grants totaling approximately 15 million dollars a month are made to these people. It is estimated that the State of Illinois will have an annual welfare budget of one billion dollars by 1970 unless the present trend of unemployment is reversed. At this stage, communal concern becomes more than just a regard for wasted talent. The problems of undereducated people make them a public liability, and their lack of funds becomes a public debt placing a severe financial burden upon the community in which they reside (4).

What is the answer? In a word, education. The greatest increase in employment opportunities between now and 1975 will be in the professional and technical fields. Gains are expected in skilled, clerical, and service occupations also. Most employers now require new workers to possess a high school diploma, because those completing secondary education will more probably be able to adjust to the changing demands characteristic of a progressing economy. In a sense the employer is thinking along the lines of Edna St. Vincent Millay, who, in "Conversation at Midnight," says (5):

> All creatures to survive adapt themselves
>   to the changing conditions under which they live;
> If they can grow new faculties
>   to meet the new necessity, they thrive;
> Otherwise not; the inflexible organism,
>   however much alive today,
> Is tomorrow extinct.*

The inability of some persons to adapt to change results in their falling by the way, in their extinction relative to continued employment. Obviously an employer engaged in a competitive market must select only those persons who will not hinder the effectiveness or efficiency of his organization. Thus, he is obliged to hire only those whose success appears predictable.

Predictive success must become a reality for more slum children if their opportunity as citizens is not to be forfeited; if our society is to maintain its philosophy of equality; if we are to win the war on poverty. Already many fine efforts are under way to improve inner-city education, with school, government, and private and community groups working together. Hopefully, other unique measures of helping slumdwellers, suggested in this text, might enhance positive outcomes. Several basic directional recommendations for boards of education, teacher training institutions, professional education associations, and community groups should be emphasized here.

---

* From *Conversation at Midnight* by Edna St. Vincent Millay and Norma Millay Ellis, p. 31. Copyright 1964, Harper & Row, Publishers, Inc. Reprinted by permission.

BOARDS OF EDUCATION

Teachers newly assigned to the central city need a program of inservice training that begins before the regular school term—what might be called a *preface plan*. Otherwise, the high incidence of staff turnover and professional dropout may be expected to continue. For most beginners, inservice assistance comes too late—at a time when some are beset by insurmountable difficulties, others have given up, and many have capitulated to the view that slum pupils are hopeless dolts. An entirely different outcome might be anticipated were a four to six week workshop with pay available preceding the fall semester. During workshop sessions new personnel would become familiar with community mores and behavioral norms, difficulties in classroom management, techniques for working with slow learners, methods of conferring with low-income parents, and the expectations of teacher role. There would be opportunities to observe motivation and incentive patterns in pupils, to participate in situations requiring disciplinary action, and to encounter supportive staff performance in resolving pupil difficulty.

Workshop progress might be greatly facilitated if a sample group of slum pupils are available, as their presence offers a prospect for at least the following: demonstration lessons by experienced teachers; personal interviews regarding values and life goals; exposure to language and speech patterns which govern communication. A sample student population also provides new teachers a chance to experience instructional success in a real situation before later confronting larger classes of their own. With this preface of experiences for persons assigned to "difficult" schools, there is reason to believe we might improve instruction and teacher attitude, increase staff satisfaction and tenure.

The board of education can also assist classroom teachers by providing an adequate number of supportive staff members. One guidance counselor per 600 slum pupils is not ample; one nurse per 2,000 students is an inadequate ratio; one psychologist or one social worker for every 1,000 children is insufficient. Yet these are the prevailing figures in the low-income districts of large cities. In the slum there are multi-problem youngsters whose families as well as they themselves require large amounts of talent, energy, and time from special service personnel. Many of the difficulties which require attention in poor neighborhoods could be substantially alleviated were more supportive specialists available for referral. When the budget is being planned, extraordinary consideration should be given where evidence indicates that an obvious increase of personnel is warranted.

In addition to a well-trained faculty, each child is entitled to an appropriate curriculum. Historically the high school has been considered an intermediate institution designed to equip only those students planning to attend college. For many years this socially accepted focus permitted schools a margin of error in planning curriculum as long as there were jobs available to the uneducated. Today, however, the inability of our technological society to make full use of an unskilled population narrows the margin to a point where the repercussions of each failure can be felt throughout the entire country. We now recognize that the provision of identical courses for all pupils is not equality of education and that noncollege-bound youngsters need and deserve instruction which will qualify them for a position in the labor market upon graduation. Only 5 percent of all high school graduates complete a vocational program, even though over half of all graduates are not college bound (6). For the schools to persuade increasing numbers of pupils to elect vocational courses may represent a healthy shift in educational objectives, but there is some doubt as to whether the actual curriculum is meeting occupational needs.

For example, reliance upon separate vocational schools to prepare many of the pupils not planning to attend college has usually been unsuccessful. This judgment is based on a 1964 Project Dropout study of school systems in the nation's 128 largest cities. Results show that while the aggregate of high schools in 1963 graduated 70.8 percent of the pupils who three years earlier (1960) were enrolled in grade 10, only 51 percent of vocational pupils in the same class remained to graduate. These findings lend credence to the assertion that, generally, vocational education has been a dumping ground for nonacademic pupils (7).

Under the Vocational Education Act of 1963, federal monetary assistance is available to school systems for developing new viable curriculums designed to meet manpower needs. In the slum especially, much of our future success will be contingent upon whether we offer such courses as barbering, cosmetology, valet service, duplicating services, painting, decorating and furniture refinishing, lawn and garden care, small appliance repair, automotive mechanics, file clerking, family services, food preparation, and laundering. Only as we affect the educational transition from a nonsensical experience to one of interest and relevance will we be able to increase the prospect of preparing many children of the poor to function in a society of specialization.

TEACHER TRAINING INSTITUTIONS

The responsibility for preparing urban educators is not exclusive to the metropolitan institution. Certainly the geographical location of certain colleges and universities render infeasible any attempt to prepare urban specialists through preservice and student teaching experiences. However, each teacher training institution can devote some attention to problems of inner-city instruction through course offerings in human development, social psychology, urban sociology, cultural anthropology, and methods of reading. Most new staff members assigned to classrooms serving the culture of poverty could be immeasurably more effective and confident if they possessed even a modicum of understanding regarding customs and values of low-income families; structure, influence and behavior of adolescent peer groups; educational strengths emerging from life in an extended family; manner and media for helpful communication with parents; diagnosis of causation underlying academic weakness; the indigenous system of incentive factors affecting motivation and discipline; and the mechanisms through which children of the poor can most positively be influenced. To the extent that the teacher lacks information about these dimensions of low-income life, there tends to be a diminution in the relevance of instruction, length of teacher tenure, and degree of job satisfaction.

Many centers of higher education are remiss in their obligation to prepare prospective instructors for intelligent confrontation of classroom disorder and pupil misconduct. By evading the disruption issue and maintaining silence regarding disciplinary problems, professors inadvertently contribute to the feelings of guilt and failure of those prospective teachers who later accept all acts of student misbehavior as a personal affront. In propounding the doctrine that pupil disrespect is usually a reflection of teacher inefficiency, others deny new personnel an access to assistance, since seeking help appears tantamount to admission of failure. As in a slum school there are few master teachers to turn to, it is not strange that a number of beginners unwittingly perpetuate inappropriate methods of class control to the disadvantage of all concerned. Many inexperienced staff members are quick to admit their ignorance and consternation regarding teacher response alternatives to class disruption. Therefore, to provide instruction in this neglected area, it would seem appropriate for preservice training to use films, role playing, demonstrations and discussions to lessen the chance of teacher failure.

To instruct the many differing personalities in the classroom effectually, teachers must be familiar with learning types, personal styles, and pace of accommodation. Moreover, the helpful leader needs to know how to identify talent by means other than paper and pencil tests, how to give open-book exams, how to diagnose pupil difficulty rather than merely assess degree of error (8). Skill in remediation techniques and diagnostic practices are perhaps two of the most obvious abilities of an outstanding teacher. The ability to conduct a meaningful conference with parents is a powerful tool that too few teachers possess. Although almost all faculty members realize the importance of techniques of conducting conferences, colleges seldom offer prospective educators any training in this context. Finally, wise selection and use of evaluative measures that relate to personal growth rather than communal progress identifies an effective mentor. If we expect slum school personnel to meet all of the criteria mentioned above, we need also expect higher education to be more relevant to the task of adequately preparing those who would teach (9).

LOCAL TEACHER ASSOCIATIONS

Professional teacher associations have a responsibility to their inner-city membership to provide the board of education with reliable up-to-date information about school and pupil needs in all geographic neighborhoods of the city. If only the system average or modal situation (for example, class size) is reported as a base for board action, it is unlikely that slum educators will receive assistance, even when their class size far exceeds pupil-teacher ratio in other schools. Similarly, when any faculty sustains a need for increased special services, class materials, and remedial instruction, the local association would be remiss in its duty were no attempt made to gain the attention of those exercising budget control. Equitable working conditions should be a major objective of teacher organizations in their attempt to gain satisfactory circumstances for all members, in districts of low or middle income alike. Unless this is an operational goal, an objective toward which genuine effort is expended, there is little advantage in associational affiliation for slum teachers.

Because one function of the local association is to foster professional growth and direction for teacher improvement, such associations can choose no more fruitful an area of influence than inservice training. In more cases than not, the questionable relevance and quality of inservice training can be attributed to the fact that responsibility for its course is delegated to someone whose schedule is already overburdened. Seldom would a teachers association that requested an opportunity to assume partial responsibility for planning the content of inservice training be rejected by school leadership. After considering those aspects of learning in which personnel desire improvement, the association can carefully plan agendas for several one-day sessions during the school year. At these meetings, each staff member might choose to participate in one of several alternative groups with varying topical concerns, such as evaluation, remediation, conducting conferences with parents, and understanding the peer group. In every case, an attempt would be made to improve teacher readiness.

If we are to encourage professional ethics, dependability and the type of competence desired for our membership, it seems only suitable to give careful attention to the selection of persons who assume responsibility for working with student teachers. A candidate in a slum school should be placed only with an experienced instructor who respects all pupils, believes that every child can learn, and does a first-rate job in the classroom. To choose a coordinating teacher simply because he has remained in a low-income institution over a period of time is to employ an improper basis of election. Survival value and professional efficiency are not always synonymous. Working in conjunction with the public school personnel department and the university student teaching bureau, association leaders should select supervising teachers of exemplary attitude and behavior. In doing so, the profession performs an invaluable service to candidates by ensuring respected direction during the field experience and promising the probability of future classroom success.

For some time, educators have hoped that neighborhoods of low financial status might develop a measure of indigenous leadership, that able slumdwellers might become teachers in their own communities. However, few children of the poor attend college and even those who do rarely return as adults to the environment of their youth. Perhaps the principal reason why slum scholars aspiring to be teachers will never enter a classroom of their own is lack of money. Thistlewaite's study (10) of persons ranking in the upper third on Merit Scholarship Qualifying Examinations showed that the greatest college dropout loss occurred among low-income pupils. Whereas the largest proportion of Merit Scholars come from homes in which the annual family income exceeds $15,000, the laboring class produces only one Merit Scholar per 3.5 million of its members. Only 5 percent of slum children currently attend college or avail themselves of other forms of higher education (11). What more appropriate group could there be to champion the cause of scholarships for poor youngsters, who though intellectually able are likely to be denied financial help, than teachers, whose vocational objective is to develop human potential? A public service would be rendered were local contingencies to carefully select promising young leaders from the classroom, encourage these children, and assist them in securing college scholarships. In some cases it might be feasible for an association to create its own "teacher scholarship fund."

NATIONAL EDUCATION ASSOCIATION

The National Education Association should establish a slum school project that would function as a production center of inservice and teacher training materials. Films and publications would be prepared to foster understandings related to classroom discipline, its alternative measures and outcomes; effective techniques of conducting conferences with low-income parents; the slum community, its values and behavioral patterns; life and educational potential in the extended family; structure, influence and function of peer groups; and motivating-teaching the slow learner. These materials based on research and practice could be available to colleges and universities for preservice courses and to metropolitan school systems for programs of inservice education.

A substantial amount of the research about disadvantaged children remains sterile in the sense that it rarely reaches those persons who could most implement its findings; namely, classroom teachers. However, difficulty of dissemination is not the sole deterrent. Most teachers are not research oriented and rarely receive any translation of study outcomes in direct terms for instructional change. Therefore, perhaps the most effectual slum project staff would be composed of persons trained in educational psychology and curriculum development, whose sophistication in teaching and research would enable them to use study results as a valuable basis of information in their production tasks.

A corollary function of the slum project should be the provision of consultation service for school systems seeking to initiate or improve inner-city inservice training programs. Periodic institutes would be feasible to better equip local leaders responsible for inservice development. These sessions could be designed to assist in the structuring of programs and to demonstrate effective usage of project materials. The consultation activities would, however, be secondary to the principal aim of production. The time is past when merely giving wide attention to the problem of undereducated persons could be considered a legitimate primary goal. Today only the myopic are unaware of the problem; most cities now seek tangible assistance rather than after-dinner speakers.

Apart from establishing a special Inner City project, the National Education Association should seriously consider its role in helping educators of slum classes obtain adequate teaching materials. A continuous lament is voiced regarding the dearth of textbooks—in reading and social studies especially—having any relation whatsoever to the experiential patterns of culturally deprived children. Then too, in classes which sustain a high incidence of reading retardation, progress is less likely if available materials are written at only one level of difficulty. According to some publishers, the reticence to produce reading materials that relate to the life space of a slum audience can be attributed to a risk factor: sales and market are limited.

The National Education Association, representing a membership of nearly a million, should attempt to generate publisher interest in this field by encouragement and, if necessary, through survey evidence indicating sales potential for a given market volume. Should this strategy fail, there are a number of other possibilities of action. Most major cities are now working independently to create materials appropriate for their own slum schools. However, limitations on the time, personnel and expenditure allocated for these tasks usually cause the result to be a cursory set of mimeographed guides leaving much to be desired. During the interim between the present and such time as publishers realize a commitment to this forgotten child audience, the National Education Association (or some combination of its components) might consider establishing a joint production center where, under the leadership of subject matter specialists, at least a modicum of well-structured reading materials could be published. Again, this would be an interim measure, a departure from policy in order to fill the gap as no other organization might—and only until more commercial publishers enter the field. Helping children would be the major outcome; such a program would also bring the National Education Association into a position of favor with teachers in the central city, whom in many respects this organization now fails to serve.

COMMUNITY EFFORTS

School orientation can be reinforced or repudiated by community influence, for only as education is valued will it be pursued. Especially is this true with reference to minority groups who find their communities to be an area for either equity or discrimination. For example, among Negro dropouts aged 18 to 21, there is a 21 percent unemployment rate; among Negro high school graduates in the same age range an unemployment rate of 17 percent obtains. These statistics explain in part one rationale for low aspiration: completion of high school seems to be of negligible value in seeking employment (12). The community must soon come to the aid of another pupil element—those who need to see a closer relationship between the world of work and the world of the classroom if they are to remain in school. By sponsoring participation in work-study programs, responsible business and industrial leaders have the possibility of generating considerable motivation, goal-orientation and vocational competence that the school alone cannot produce (13).

Numerous civic and private organizations also have a role in stimulating educational achievement. Fraternal groups like the Kiwanis, Rotary, Lions, and Elks have functioned successfully as "big brothers" to disadvantaged youth by providing trips, distributing tickets to ball games, assisting in the location of jobs, initiating scholarships, absorbing expenses for eyeglasses and other health aids. The Y.M.C.A., community centers and fraternal youth groups have been generous in providing free membership entries and opportunities to take part in outings, sporting events and special entertainment. Community welfare and employment agencies are, of course, constantly working to establish the possibility of individual advance and independence. Church associations have helped by establishing supervised and tutorial study centers where a quiet place to read is available as well as adult help should it be desired. In some districts able members of the Parent Teachers Association are indirectly improving instruction by working as teacher aides, assuming many clerical and monitorial tasks. Each of these collective benefactors is instrumental in lessening the chances that slum children will grow up to become slum adults.

The war on poverty cannot be won without a concerted attack on ignorance. Most slumdwellers have a desire to cast off the life style they now endure but find that their economic inability to function in a technological society forms fetters from which they cannot escape. They need more than aspiration, hope and the will to succeed; they need education, learning, the power of thought. The future of the slum must not be a repetition of its past and will not be if each of us works toward making good our nation's commitment to equal opportunity. In the words of Robert Frost, we "have promises to keep."

RESOURCES

(1) Riessman, Frank, *The Culturally Deprived Child* (New York: Harper & Row, Publishers, 1962), p. 1.

108   Prospects

(2)   Flanagan, John C., *Project Talent News* (University of Pittsburgh),
      Vol. 3, No. 1 (March 1964), p. 1.

(3)   Strom, Robert D., "School Dropouts in a World of Work," *Cali-
      fornia Teachers Association Journal,* Vol. 60, No. 4 (October
      1964), pp. 4–6.

(4)   Strom, Robert D., "The Dropout in Relation to Family Affect and
      Effect," *Journal of Home Economics,* Vol. 56, No. 5 (May 1964),
      pp. 299–304.

(5)   Millay, Edna St. Vincent and Norma Millay Ellis, *Conversation
      at Midnight* (New York: Harper & Row, Publishers, 1964), p. 31.

(6)   Venn, Grant, *Man, Education and Work* (Washington, D.C.:
      American Council on Education, 1964), p. 167.

(7)   Strom, Robert D., "School Dropouts in a World of Work," *Cali-
      fornia Teachers Association Journal,* Vol. 60, No. 4 (October
      1964), pp. 4–6.

(8)   Horrocks, John E., "Culture Free Tests of Intelligence," *Assess-
      ment of Behavior* (Columbus, Ohio: Charles E. Merrill Books,
      Inc., 1964), pp. 271–96.

(9)   Conant, James B., *The Education of American Teachers* (New
      York: McGraw-Hill Book Co., 1963), 275 pp.

(10) National School Public Relations Association, *Education USA*
      (Washington, D.C.: the Association, a Department of the National
      Education Association, December 12, 1963), p. 57.

(11) Panel on Educational Research and Development for the Presi-
      dent's Science Advisory Committee, "The Deprived and the Segre-
      gated," *Innovation and Experiment in Education* (Washington,
      D.C.: Government Printing Office, March 1964), pp. 29–38.

(12) Strom, Robert D., "Education: Key to Economic Equality for the
      Negro," *Journal of Negro Education,* Vol. 34 (Fall 1965).

(13) Conant, James B., *Slums and Suburbs* (New York: McGraw-Hill
      Book Co., 1961), "Schools and Jobs in the Big City," pp. 33–53.

INDEXES

Index of Names

111

Index of Subjects